A Salamander Book

© 1989 Salamander Books Ltd
Published by Tetra Press, 3001 Commerce St, Blacksburg, VA 24060

ISBN 1-56465-151-7

All correspondence concerning the content of this volume should be addressed to Tetra Press.

Credits

Editor: Jo Finnis
Designer: Philip Gorton
Photographer: Marc Henrie
Illustrations: Ray Hutchins
US consultants: Hal and Mary Sundstrom; Seymour N Weiss
Color origination: Bantam Litho Ltd
Filmsetting: SX Composing, Rayleigh, Essex
Printed in Belgium

Contents

Introduction	10
A history of the breed	14
The Chow Chow puppy	22
The adult Chow Chow	36
The smooth Chow Chow	46
Showing your Chow Chow	52
Breeding your Chow Chow	70
Health care	84
Appendix	92

Author

Diana Phillips has been with Chow Chows since the 1940s. Her mother, Mrs Doris Claxton, was a well-known Championship Show judge of Chows, and her sister, Miss Gillian Claxton, is also a well-known Championship Show judge.
Diana judged her first show in 1963 and her first Championship Show appointment was in 1977. She has also judged Chows at Championship Shows in Germany, Holland and France and has awarded CACs in Shar Pei in Holland.
Diana believes in breeding a healthy Chow for a long life and was the breeder and exhibitor of the well-known veteran, Chanoyu Midnight Sirius who won a record 114 Best Veteran awards. Diana is a long-standing member of the committee of the Chow Chow Club in the UK.

A DOG OWNER'S GUIDE TO

THE CHOW CHOW

Tetra❂Press

16046

Guidelines On Canine Nutrition

There is much misunderstanding and misinformation about canine nutrition. Many pet owners search continually for the perfect food. Some owners add supplements in the mistaken belief they can make the accepted food "better". This can result in a harmful result, quite the opposite of the good that was intended.

Many pet foods advertise that their foods meet or "exceed" minimum nutritional requirements. Excesses of such nutrients as protein, phosphorous and sodium may be very harmful to the health of the kidney over time. Too much salt (sodium) may also contribute to heart disease. Your veterinarian or breeder is best qualified to prescribe a food that contains the optimum or "just right" level of nutrients to meet the needs of your dog. Avoiding foods containing excesses is an excellent way to practice preventative health care.

DIETARY MANAGEMENT

What your dog eats must satisfy its body's need for energy and for protein, vitamins, minerals and

water. The level of these nutrients needed to provide a balanced diet will vary widely according to age, activity level, temperament and environment.

Noted veterinary scientists Dr. Mark L. Morris, Sr. and Dr. Mark L. Morris, Jr., pioneers in research in animal nutrition, developed the concept of "dietary management," which is the daily lifelong control of food intake to meet the changing unique requirements of both the healthy and diseased animal in order to extend the quality and length of life.

GROWTH

The objective is to feed a diet that provides the increased nutrients needed for maximum disease resistance and optimal musculoskeletal growth.

Recommendations

1. Feed a diet that contains the recommended nutrient levels (see table 1) and specifies that it has been proven adequate.
2. Feed puppies twice daily until 12 months of age.

3. Do not supplement with anything — particularly vitamins or minerals. Supplements are not required if a nutritionally adequate diet is fed. Supplements will not improve a nutritionally adequate diet; they often upset the nutrient balance of the diet.

Considerations
1. Overfeeding puppies may result in skeletal disease or obesity. The development of obesity during growth predisposes to it later in life.
2. A poorly digestible diet may cause diarrhea, increased susceptibility to infectious diseases, predisposition to bloat later in life by increasing food intake and stomach distention, and decreased mature size.

Diets of Choice: High-energy, highly-digestible diet, balanced for growth.

MAINTENANCE

The objective is to provide a diet that supplies optimal amounts of all nutrients for maximum health and longevity by preventing the excesses present in many commercial pet foods. Prolonged consumption by adult dogs of diets adequate for growth, or "all purpose" diets containing excessive amounts of protein, calcium, phospherous, sodium, or magnesium, predisposes to, and/or promotes the progression of major diseases affecting dogs such as skin, kidney, heart and vascular disease, and urolithiasis.

Recommendations
1. Feed a diet that contains the recommended nutrient levels (see table 2).
2. Feed amount necessary to maintain optimal body weight. This weight has been achieved when the dog's ribs can be *easily* felt by pressing the palm of the hand against the side of the chest. It should not be possible to see the ribs when merely observing the animal.

OLD AGE

The objective is to prolong an enjoyable life by ameliorating existing problems and slowing or preventing the development or progression of disease.

Management
1. Beginning at 8-9 years of age, feed a diet that contains the recommended nutrient levels (see table 3). This will necessitate using a properly formulated diet for older dogs.
2. Feed amount necessary to maintian optimal body weight. Many older dogs have a tendency to become less active. If caloric intake is not controlled, obesity will develop.

Considerations
1. Insure adequate physical activity to maintain muscle tone and optimal body weight, enhance circulation, and improve waste elimination.
2. Early detection and proper nutritional management will delay the onset of clinical signs and slow the progression of renal and heart failure.

Diets of Choice: Palatable, highly-digestible diet with reduced levels of protein, phosphorus, and sodium.

ORPHANS

The objective is to replace the nutrition that would normally be provided by the mother. This requires supplying a balanced nutrient source capable of supporting growth. There are several products available. Consult your veterinarian concerning type and amount of milk/replacer necessary.

REPRODUCTION

The objective is to feed a diet that provides in readily utilizable form the increased amounts of nutrients needed for gestation and maximal milk production while maintaining body weight.

Recommendations

1. Prior to breeding:
   Have your veterinarin
   a. perform a thorough physical examination.
   b. Check, and if necessary, treat for internal and external parasites.
   c. Vaccinate according to your veterinarian's recommendations so that a good immunity is passed to the young.
   d. Adjust the female to optimal body weight.

2. Particularly during the last three weeks of gestation and throughout lactation feed a diet that contains the recommended nutrient levels (see table 4) and specifies that it has been proven adequate for growth and reproduction in special feeding tests.

3. Feed the amount necessary so that optimal non-pregnant body weight increases 15-25% during gestation and is maintained during lactation. Frequently this requires meal feeding during gestation and the feeding of an excellent quality high-energy food free-choice during lactation. It is very seldom helpful or necessary to supplement this type of diet with calcium supplements.

Considerations

If "milk fever" (eclampsia) has occurred previously in the female, start the young eating solid food by three weeks of age and, if necessary, supplement them with a milk replacer. Diets of Choice: Highly-digestible, high-energy diet balanced with reproduction.

Table 1: Diet Characteristics Recommended for Growth

Metabolizable kcal/lb	% in Food Dry Matter						
	Digestibility	Protein	Fat	Fiber	Ca	P	Sodium
greater than 1750	greater than 80	greater than 29	greater than 17	less than 5	1.0-1.8	0.8-1.6	0.3-0.7

Table 2: Diet Characteristics Recommended for Maintenance

% in Food Dry Matter					
Digestibility	Protein	Fat	Ca	P	Sodium
greater than 75	15-20	greater than 8	0.5-0.9	0.4-0.8	0.2-0.5

Table 3: Diet Characteristics Recommended for Aged Dogs

Metabolizable kcal/lb	% in Food Dry Matter						
	Digestibility	Protein	Fat	Fiber	Ca	P	Sodium
greater than 1750	greater than 80	14-21	greater than 10	5-10	0.5-0.9	0 4-0.7	0.2-0.4

Table 4: Diet Characteristics Recommended for Reproduction

Metabolizable kcal/lb	% in Food Dry Matter						
	Digestibility	Protein	Fat	Fiber	Ca	P	Sodium
greater than 1750	greater than 80	greater than 29	greater than 17	less than 5	1.0-18	0.8-1.6	0.3-07

Introduction

Is the Chow the right breed for you?

There is nothing so attractive as the little bundle of fluff and fun we call a Chow puppy. But, even though it reminds so many people of a toy teddy-bear, we must remember that this cuddly creature is no toy but a living, growing animal with its own needs and its own developing character. Owning any dog brings with it ongoing responsibilities which should not be lightly entered into. A Chow is a most rewarding and wonderful companion but it is probably the most unconventional of all breeds. It is most important that you understand the innate character, needs and behaviour of a Chow and match them with your own expectation of your prospective pet, since a mismatch would be a disaster for all.

This pretty little puppy will grow into a medium-sized, dignified, intelligent adult. A grown Chow will be approximately at knee-height to the average person. His squarely balanced body contains a power which can be likened to being in 'four-wheel drive'. He will need time and attention paid to his training to control this power. His high grade of intelligence and reasoning means that he requires to build his loving relationship with his owner in order to respond. A Chow does not respond without seeing the reason for the response. He can be self-willed almost to obstinacy, but his wishes usually comply with those of his master or mistress. He is often referred to as a 'one-man dog' because he is so utterly loyal and devoted to his family and chosen friends.

Below: *Byhorn Cedar at Chanoyu makes an attractive picture standing in her sunny garden, but she can be a handful too!*

Right: *Happy and fully alert, this Chow is thoroughly enjoying a game in the long grass of her own garden.*

A Chow's coat is one of his most attractive features. In the full glory of his coat he is beautiful in colouring and handsome in form. There is an absence of any 'doggy smell'. But owning any long-coated breed of dog involves regular attention to grooming or the coat will soon become matted.

He will quietly guard your house and garden, the famous scowling expression giving a forbidding appearance to unwelcome callers. He is a wonderful watchdog, only barking when necessary. Intelligently he quickly learns who is friend and who is a suspected foe. But he is not a dog to be chained and encouraged to be a ferocious guard.

The Chow is happy in town or country providing he can have sufficient exercise. Your country Chow may find enough exercise within his own garden only needing walks as a mental stimulant, but the town Chow must have his daily constitutional. Moderate amounts of exercise are required, not as much as the larger, sporting breeds. Exercise off the lead is not normally encouraged as his independence can lead him astray! Also beware if you live near poultry or sheep! It is most important that any home area in which the Chow will be is securely fenced.

If you have young children a Chow is an ideal companion and guard for them. Chows love children. But, whilst they will accept more roughness from a child than from an adult, it must be your responsibility to see that your child treats the Chow with kindness and thoughtfulness at all times. Rebuke the child who is misbehaving with the dog, or vice-versa, and never allow teasing or rough play. Mutual respect will make for mutual love and devotion.

The Chow is a long-lived breed. They are slow to mature, many not reaching their best until about four or five years old. They are mostly still young in their ways at 12 and many live till about 14 or 15. Are you prepared to devote so many years into the future to your dog? Their loyalty means that you should be prepared to enter into your contract with them for the duration of their life.

Do you have the time to spare? A puppy will occupy the greater part of the day in caring, feeding, lessons and companionship. The older dog will also take a part of every day for companionship and the attention he requires and deserves. A Chow is not there to feed, clean up after and forget. He needs your time and will richly reward you for it.

Are you prepared to wait a while for your puppy? Chows are not the easiest of dogs to breed and demand usually exceeds supply. This is good for the breed, since it usually weeds out the impatient or unsuitable owner. Once you feel that you would like to own a Chow it will give you time to learn and appreciate the basic character and needs of the breed.

If you are looking for a dog which will instantly obey without question, which will do parlour tricks, will be a cheap burglar alarm or a smart status symbol, then forget it now. But if you are looking for a faithful, devoted, intelligent and handsome companion, then read on. You are then ready to own a Chow — or rather to be owned by one! Once a Chow owner, always a Chow owner.

Above: *Tanlap Titbit in happy companionship with his devoted young owners, Angharad and David.*

Below: *A happy and alert group of both smooth and rough coated puppies wondering what the big, wide world has in store.*

13

Chapter One

A HISTORY OF THE BREED

THE ORIGINS

In a remote, mysterious period of evolution appeared the animal we now call a Chow Chow. Without any doubt it is one of our most ancient breeds of dog. Historians have found chronicles dating as far back as the 11th century BC which describe the 'Tartar dog' or 'Foreign Chow', clearly showing that the unique characteristics were then present. The dogs are described as 'heavily built with harsh, bristly hair, absolutely straight back legs and blue tongues'. Evolution and subsequent domestication had obviously taken place before that time.

In the genealogical tree of carnivores, the last to separate were the canines and the ursines. During the Miocene period, about 28 to 12 million years ago, there appeared a late descendant, the Hemicyon, which was an intermediate between dog and bear, moderate in size and in many respects very dog-like. Its direct descendant was the Simicyon, an animal which varied in size from a fox to a small bear. These animals inhabited the sub-arctic regions and an advancing Ice Age drove them southwards towards Siberia and Northern Mongolia. Apart from the Chow's obvious bear-like features, it is interesting to note that the Chow shares with the small bears of Tibet and Manchuria the characteristic blue-black tongue, the broad skull, short muzzle and square body. These are ursine rather than lupine features. Final and conclusive proof is provided by the animals' dentition. Whereas the normal dog-group has 42 teeth, the Hemicyons and Simicyons have 44 to 46. The Chow also has 44 teeth, although they usually lose the extra two in their adult dentition. The Chow, or an ancestor very like it, was probably established on the high, cold steppes of Mongolia many, many years before the evolution of ape-man into homo sapiens.

THE CHOW ARRIVES IN CHINA

China was frequently invaded by the barbaric tribes on its Northern borders. These tribes, the Tartars and Mongols, were accompanied by their 'war dogs'. At this time the word 'Mastiff' was often used but not with its current meaning. 'Mastiff', as used then, indicated a dog of size, strength and hunting ability and was used indiscriminately by writers and translators irrespective of the breed of dog. The Tartar war dogs were described as of 'lion-like appearance, large, powerful and distinguished by black tongues'. Records show that the Emperor Wu Wang (1122-1116 BC) received a tribute from the enemy of a great number of their dogs described as 'of great strength with plenty of hair and mostly red in colour'. In spite of the destruction of Chinese literature ordered by the Emperor Chin Shih in 255 BC, numerous references still remain which refer to dogs being brought into China by the various barbaric tribes living on the Northern borders and which are either named as the 'Foreign Chow' or whose description fits the Chow so accurately. There is the persistent link of the blue or blue-black tongue and the unique stiff back legs; also the black gums and lips and the mention of the lips not overlapping but just touching — a feature which gives the Chow its typical aloof look.

The 'Tartar war-dog' or 'Foreign Chow' was found by the Chinese to be 'worthy of the use of man' and was highly valued for hunting, herding and guarding. Emperors and noblemen kept the Chow in luxurious accommodation. The Emperor Ling Ti bred Chows as members of the Imperial Household which were fed on the best rice and meat by an army of servants, had a military escort, slept on rich carpets and were awarded high courtly titles and decorations such as the Order of Kai Fu (Viceroy). These Chows had the double purpose of guarding the Palace and looking handsome and dignified. Emperors of the Tang dynasty had hunting kennels of 25,000 couples of 'hounds' of true Chow type. In the Book of Rites (7th century BC) the 'foreign chow' was classified as a hunting dog used to attack wolves and leopards. As a hunter the Chow had remarkable powers of scent, clever tactics on the line and great strength. This strength is evident in

Below: *Pottery Chow Chow from the Han Period (c 200 BC). The strong harness indicates the immense strength of the Chow.*

Above: *Mrs Scaramanga's four Champions. From the left: Theem Kwy, Red Craze, Wiggles and Hah-Kwy. Painted circa 1905.*

the use of the harness shown on the ceramic figurines from the tombs of the Han period (206 BC -220AD) where the dog is 'on a leash attached to a curious kind of body-strap connected by a strap in the front and bound into an iron ring over the back to which the leash is attached, and by their very stoutness indicate that the dogs were extremely powerful'. These models were buried with their dead masters to ward off the 'evil influences of obnoxious spirits'. In the province of Yunnan the dogs used to hunt the musk deer were described as 'Chow-dogs of larger size and weight, very active and sure-footed'. During this period there are many references in early Chinese chronicles which are easily recognizable as the Chow. 'Square dogs that look fierce, like lions whom they resemble much by neck, being well covered with hair, face, colour and nails; falling upon bears and boars. They seldom do bark except in their hunting chase, and then they follow their game through woods, thickets, thorns and most difficult places.' 'Strange animals and utterly different from any other breed being of a suspicious nature, surly and hostile to strangers but exceedingly courageous.' There is also in existence a painting of a

Chinese Imperial household of about 2,000 years ago which clearly shows a Chow lying under a table. This chow has a perfectly groomed red coat and has the same scowling expression as the Chows of today.

So far references to the Chow have shown its colour as red or black. But in the isolated, rocky mountains of Northern China, Manchuria and Mongolia, the monks in the Lamaistic Buddhist monasteries were breeding blue Chows. The early Chinese were skilled in the genetics of colour breeding and it must have taken them a considerable time to stabilize this dilution of black to the constant perfection of pale blue which they attained. These blue Chows were used to guard and protect the monastery, to herd the cattle and as hunting dogs and they were jealously guarded by the monks. The Chow in his restraining harness resembled greatly the sacred lion, the defender of the faithful with the harness which signified servitude to Buddha. These blue dogs were

Above: *Ch Young Cheng of Amwell, a two year-old bitch belonging to the famous Amwell kennel of Lady Faudel Phillips.*

distinguished not only by their colour but are also recorded as being larger in size and with better bone than those outside the monasteries.

With the ending of the Tang dynasty came an increasing national poverty and, except within the monasteries, selective breeding ceased. The Imperial hunts were no more. The original pure-bred Chow remained only within the households of wealthy merchants and noblemen and the monasteries. The thrifty, commercially minded Chinese established dog-farms. The Chow was found to be useful not only for herding, hunting, sledging and guarding but it had a useful fur pelt and was also edible. Large dog-farms were set up in the Northern districts where Chows were bred for their valuable fur, the dogs being strangulated at about 10 to 12 months old so as not to damage the pelt. Strict society rules demanded that 'over a tunic trimmed with dog or sheep skin it is forbidden to wear a second tunic for this is done to show off the beauty of the costume'. In Manchuria when a peasant girl married she received a dowry of a team of six Chows as a foundation for her farm.

The flesh of the Chow was a desirable substitute for mutton and the provinces of Kwantung and Kwan-si specialized in breeding for table use. In Canton the dogs were fed on a special rice diet to improve the flavour. Black dogs were said to be especially nutritious. Tender puppies killed at nine months were reserved for the wealthy whilst the poorer classes ate the adult dogs. Chow's tongue was a delicacy thought to have healing properties. Dog was eaten in the Autumn with oleaginous grain and was especially mentioned to be eaten at the Chinese Feast of A-chee. In 1928 AD a law was passed in the province of Peking forbidding the eating of dog flesh. In spite of this, some of the older Chinese are said still to know where to purchase this and it is sold under the name of 'fragrant meat'. To this day dog is still eaten in South Korea where it is customarily served as medallions of meat on a bed of onions. Could this be why the Chow retains his characteristic scowl as though he has preserved a grievance against life?

17

THE CHOW TRAVELS WEST

The first European person to mention and describe the Chow was Marco Polo, who visited China as a guest of the Great Mogul in the 13th century and who wrote about them in his account of his travels. But the Chow was unknown in the Western world until the late 18th century when it was brought back as a curiosity by sailors and merchants in the Clipper ships of the East India Company. Writing in his book *The Natural History and Antiquities of Selborne*, the Rev Gilbert White describes in accurate detail the import of a pair of puppies from Canton by a young gentleman of the East India Company. These were 'of the Chinese breed of Canton such as are fattened in this country to be eaten'. He goes on to say 'the hind legs are usually straight without any bend at the hock. The eyes are jet black, small and piercing, the inside of the lip and mouths the same colour and the tongues blue.' Clearly these wre definitely Chows, probably amongst the first in England as this was in the early 1780's. During the early 19th century a few Chows were brought in as curiosities. There is reference to an Oriental dog with thick red coat and blue-black tongue coming from China, several Chows were housed in London Zoo in the Wild Dog area and in 1865 Queen Victoria was presented with some Chows which were kept in cages at Windsor.

But an interest in Chows for breeding and exhibition must have begun in 1879 when a black Chow bitch named Chinese Puzzle came to England. The following year she was exhibited at the Crystal Palace dog show by her owner Mr W K Taunton. It is interesting to note, in the light of our present breed standard, that she measured 16in (40.6cm) at shoulder and weighed 32lb (14.5kg). In 1884 the Earl of Lonsdale imported a Chow and three years later he gave the

Above: *Terracotta model of Ch Cheefoo who was the dam of Ch Akbar. Model made in 1936 in France by Richard Fath.*

Right: *Ch Choonam Hung Kwong. The only Chow to have won Best in Show at Crufts (1936). He also won 44 CC's.*

Marchioness of Huntley a dog named Peridot. She then bred a Chow named Peridot II which was the foundation for Lady Granville Gordon's kennel. Lady Granville Gordon was instrumental in getting the Kennel Club to recognize the breed as a Chow Chow rather than as a 'Foreign Dog'. She also owned the first blue Chows in England. Her daughter, Lady Faudel-Phillips, later founded the famous Amwell kennels and became the leading breeder and exhibitor until about 1898. In 1890 the first Chow was exhibited in America. This was 'Takya' owned by Miss A C Derby.

One of the most important years in the history of the Chow must surely be 1895. Four important events occurred. Champion Chow VIII became the first ever Chow Champion, Peridot II was awarded Best in Show at the LKA Championship show, the Chow Chow Club was formed and the breed standard was formulated based on Ch Chow VIII.

Since then the breeding and exhibition of Chows has gone on apace. Mrs Jarrett of Philadelphia founded the first American Chow kennel and got recognition for the breed from the American Kennel Club. Chinese Chum was exported to Mrs Proctor of America where he became an American Champion and sired many American Champions including Am Ch Black Cloud and Am Ch Night of Asia, which were the foundation for her 'Blue Dragon' kennels. In 1906 the American Chow Club was founded. This was followed in 1924 by the foundation of the French Chow Chow Club by Mme Mareschal (revived after the last war by Mme Yvonne Diot). Also in 1924 we have the first entry of a Chow in the German Stud Book.

Gradually the Chow's lovable character became more widely known and from the 1920's the popularity of the breed steadily increased and is still increasing to this day. Quite a number of well-known, not to say famous, people have owned Chows. In our own Royal Family others as well as Queen Victoria have had Chows as pets. Queen Alexandra, in her own words 'mad about animals', was presented with a Chow by the King's Equerry, Sir Henry Knollys, which had been brought some 12,000 miles to Sandringham by a Captain in the Indian Army. The Late Duke of Kent owned a Chow and our present Queen Elizabeth II has fond childhood memories of her relatives' Chows. Statesmen too have owned Chows — Lloyd George owned two Chows and a Chow lived in the White House at the time of President Calvin Coolidge. The actress Sarah Bernhardt, the playwright George Bernard Shaw, Sigmund Freud, Dr Konrad Lorenz, the Rothschilds and the celebrated orchestral conductor Herbert von Karajan have all owned Chows in their time. There is a lovely description of a Chow 'Pooh-Bah' in *The Bird in the Tree* by Elizabeth Goudge who did not own a Chow but who lived in the same village as Mrs Martin (Nitram Chows) and obviously must have been fascinated by the Chow character as she describes it so accurately.

LEGENDS

It is not surprising that three of the legends I have found refer to the Chow's almost unique colour mouth and tongue. The only other canine breed which shares this peculiarity is the Chinese Shar Pei which comes from the same area and probably from similar origins. The blackness of the mouth was said to ward off evil spirits and so enhanced the Chow's reputation as a guard dog of both palaces and monasteries. Then there are two fanciful 'explanations' of how the Chow came to have this strange colour tongue. 'Many hundreds of years ago, when dog-eaters were running wild all over the country, there was a lone monk living deep in the hills who took in stray dogs for company. He was very kind to all animals and they, in turn, were very grateful for his kindness. One day the monk fell very ill and was unable to go to pick up firewood to make dinner, so all the dogs and animals banded together to do the chores. It so happened that some trees in a nearby forest were thunderstruck and left a pile of charcoal. The Chow Chow rummaged along the forest floor and picked up some of these charcoal pieces. The monkey made the meals thereafter until the monk was well again. But the tongue of the Chow Chow was stained black ever since the day he picked up the charcoal — an insignia of the good deed he did in return for the monk's generosity and protection.' Alternatively . . . 'When the world was being created, what dog was allowed to lick up all the little pieces of blue sky which fell on the earth when the stars were set in their places? "The Chow," said Li Fu, "and that's how he got his blue tongue." '

The last story comes not from China but from its near neighbour, Japan. Long, long ago in old Japan a samurai was travelling through a strange province. He was crossing a rugged mountainous area when darkness fell. It would have been unwise to spend the night in the open for fear of lions or wolves so, just as the sun was setting, he hurried to the only building he could find, a tumbledown ruined temple. It did not give much protection but he climbed up a ruined buttress, spread out his blanket and tried to sleep. Just before midnight he was awakened by a dreadful, unearthly howling noise. Peering down he saw in the moonlight hundreds and hundreds of cats of all shapes, colours and sizes. Straining to understand their blood-curdling howling, the samurai thought he could recognize a phrase over and over again: 'Tell it not to Shippeitaro!' 'Who or what can Shippeitaro mean?' wondered the samurai. Suddenly the cats turned tail and vanished. The next day the samurai travelled on and in the nearby village he met with people who were wailing with grief. They were weeping because that night they had to take the fairest maiden in the village to the ruined temple where she would be eaten by the evil spirits. These evil spirits were seen in the form of wild cats. The samurai asked who or what was

Shippeitaro. 'Shippeitaro is a dog — a fine dog. He is brave and strong, yet gentle with children — he belongs to the head man, our prince.' At this the samurai departed. But, 'an hour later he returned, leading the dog Shippeitaro on a lead of plaited leather. Shippeitaro was a golden colour, with a purple tongue — we would call him a chow.' The samurai put Shippeitaro into the cage instead of the maiden and he and four young men carrying the cage set off for the temple. 'Midnight came and the howling of the cats rose to a horrible crescendo . . . There was a crash as Shippeitaro beat the door open in his impatience to be out, and a sudden flash of gold as the gallant dog shot like an arrow from a bow, and grabbed the great tomcat firmly in his jaws. Then down leaped the samurai and with a great cry swept the giant tomcat's head from its shoulders with one mighty swing of his two-handed sword. The other cats were so

astonished that they forgot to run away and Shippeitaro soon put an end to them.' When the villagers heard this 'all their tears were forgotten and praise and thanksgiving were universal — the greatest praise of all going to Shippeitaro, the bravest dog in all Japan.'

THE NAME 'CHOW CHOW'

It is very difficult to say how a breed as old as the Chow came by its name. One of its original names was 'Chao' meaning 'a large, primitive, extraordinary dog of great strength' and the name 'Ao', which occurs in the 11th century BC, is probably a corruption of this. Also in the same century it is called 'Man Kou' meaning 'dog of the barbarians' or 'Tartar dog'. By AD 100 it was variously referred to as 'Mang' (dog with much hair), 'Chao' (dog of great strength) or 'Ti' (red dog). Upon reaching the western world many centuries later it was called at first the 'Foreign Dog' and then the 'Chinese Edible Dog'. But the people of the western world did not like to be reminded of its edible purpose and so adopted the name 'Chow Chow'. This may have been because various commodities brought from China were known in pidgin English as 'chow chow' or it may have been directly from the original 'Chao'.

Below left: *Ch Wat A Gal of Ukwong who became the youngest Champion of any breed when she won her title at 7½ months.*

Below: *Mrs J Egerton's famous Ch Ukwong King Solomon, holder of 78 CC's — an all-time record for any breed.*

Chapter Two

THE CHOW CHOW PUPPY

LOOKING FOR A PUPPY

By now you have probably decided that a Chow puppy is definitely for you. But wait! Are all your family agreed on that? It is most important that every member of the family is as truly enthusiastic as you are. A Chow will very soon sense whether or not he is liked and unless he is loved he will become an unhappy dog and probably a future candidate for the sadness of needing the rescue group. However, there is likely to be time to assess the feelings of your family since it is more than likely that you will have to wait quite a while to achieve your purchase. Chows are not easy to breed. Mating a bitch is certainly no guarantee of a litter, as any Chowist will tell you. During this almost inevitable waiting period, do try to become as involved as possible with Chows. Surprisingly there are probably some, not necessarily show ones, which live nearer to your home than you may think. Chowists, whether show or pet owners, are always only too pleased to show off their pride and joy to would-be new enthusiasts. You will learn just as much about day-to-day life with a Chow in the family from a pet owner as from an exhibitor.

How do you find these people? Apart from any usually rather rare local press advertisements, there are the national dog papers which sometimes show that there are Chow puppies for sale. Certainly you will get from this press details of Chow breed shows which will be more than worth while your attendance, whether or not you are hoping to show. At the shows you will make the acquaintance of many Chowists and their dogs and certainly receive much invaluable help both in purchasing your puppy and in looking after it. You will have the opportunity to be amongst the breed and make a real assessment as to whether it is truly the breed you want. The various Breed Clubs are always prepared to help the prospective new owner and can give advice on where puppies may be found and where your nearest Chow owners live. The Kennel Club in London (or your national kennel club — see Appendix) will also provide you with the names of reputable Chow breeders in your area and will give you the addresses of Breed Clubs.

Having found the person you hope to buy your puppy from, try to spend some time with them assessing both them and their Chows. What are their own dogs like? Are they well kept, well fed, happy, confident and obviously loved? Do the premises look (and smell) clean and tidy? Or does this appear to be a kennels producing for purely commercial reasons, perhaps buying in puppies of many breeds for pure commercial gain (puppy farms)? Beware of puppy farms — sentiment may cause you to feel you must rescue the pup from his surroundings (they trade on that) but if you succumb to your understandable and laudable feelings you may take on innumerable vets bills and may well have only sadness ahead.

A reputable breeder will welcome your questions and will never grudge the time spent showing you round and helping you. They will probably be asking you as many questions as you are asking them because they should be checking you out too. The breeder should be assessing your approach and attitude to the Chows, whether or not your life-style is appropriate to the Chow's needs and whether or not you have suitable surroundings for the Chow to live in. I often wonder what any prospective purchaser thinks of me, for, to hear me questioning them, anyone would think I did not want to sell the puppy! But then a responsible

breeder does not want to sell a puppy into the wrong environment. The breeder should be prepared to give you help and guidance both at the time of sale and in the future. A conscientious breeder not only wants the customer to be satisfied but also takes a real interest and concern in the continuing welfare of the dogs he or she has caused to be born into the world. The more time and thought you give at this planning stage of purchase, the more likely you are to buy a healthy, properly raised puppy from healthy, well-bred stock.

CHOOSING YOUR PUPPY

At last comes the exciting day when you can go to choose your very own puppy! The best time to choose your puppy is when the litter is six weeks old. At the age of six to nine weeks the puppy is usually a miniature version of what it will be when adult. Any later and the pup may start to grow first one way and then another so not giving a true picture of future balance. Like children, they tend to go through some awkward and gangly stages. If you are genuinely looking for a family pet only and have no ambitions either to exhibit or to breed with your pet then you have the easiest task. You will be

Below: *A beautiful large litter of blue Chow puppies born in France. Note the uniformity of colour in the litter.*

Above. *Two red smooth-coated puppies aged six weeks. The attractive black mask on red puppies disappears with age.*

able to concentrate on choosing a happy, healthy, well reared, attractive puppy without worrying about the finer breed points. But do be honest here. A pet puppy is likely to be a little cheaper to buy than a show prospect, but it does no-one any service, least of all the Chow, to find that the dog, sold genuinely as a pet, is being shown and bred from.

It is essential that you check for the health points. The puppy should be clean and sweet-smelling, with bright alert eyes. There should be no discharge from nose or eyes. The mouth should be clean with clean white (and needle-sharp!) teeth. The body should be sturdy, strong and well muscled without being grossly fat. The puppy should be active and alert, full of life and playfulness. Never force yourself on a puppy — let him come to you. Although it is quite likely that a puppy will come forward and literally choose you, do not overlook the one with a little reserve. Caution is a characteristic of the breed and a natural reserve can be mistaken for timidity. Once the puppy is secure in his new little world all will be well and he will become a steady, reliable companion. Remember that so far he knows nothing of life

but romping with his littermates and being with the security of his mother. Spend time observing the litter and you will discover whether it is caution or timidity.

Naturally you would wish to see the puppies' mother. She will give you some idea of what your puppy may look like in the future and you will be in a position to judge her temperament. But do please remember that she has given much of herself in gestating, whelping and rearing these pups. This is the very time when she looks at her very worst having completely cast her coat in addition to becoming unnaturally thin. She does not usually look like this!

I have not gone into the question of whether to purchase a dog or a bitch. Some people say bitches of any breed are more loving than dogs; some people worry about a bitch coming into season twice a year with its attendant problems. Veterinary science has progressed so that there are several ways of coping with the latter and my own

Above: *Byhorn Sorrel at Mei-Ping. The first Chow to qualify for the Pup of the Year Competition for 15 years.*

experience tells me that both sexes are equally devoted to a caring owner. Your dog will be what you make him or her. Devote time, love and attention and you will be amply repaid by either sex. So I feel that the choice of sex is immaterial; it is the character of the puppy which matters.

If you feel that there is the remotest possibility that you might wish to exhibit or breed with your dog then, in addition to all the points already mentioned, you must assess the puppy in relation to the breed standard. The breeder should be able to help you in your judgement. Place your choice of puppy four-square on a table and look to see that the overall picture is one of squareness and balance. Check the set of the teeth. They should fit closely in a scissor bite and the incisors should be set in a fairly straight line. The tongue should be blue without any suggestion of pink, although at this age the rest of the mouth and gums may not yet have attained their final pigmentation. The eyes

should be well-shaped, clean and dark. The nose should be broad and the nostrils black. The ears may not be up at this age but you should check that they are not too large nor too thin. It is important to check that the skull between the ears is not domed. The neck should be well set on the shoulders. Sturdy legs with strong bone right down to little rounded feet should not only look but also feel as straight as a die. There should be a real squareness about the space between the front legs and a lovely strong chest. The hind legs should be set in a straight line from the root of the tail to the ground. From the point of the hock to the ground should be short and parallel to one another. The whole back view should be chunky and square. The rib cage should extend well back along the body. The overall length of back should be short. The tail should be set on high and should be carried well over the back. The coat colour will not be much of a guide to the final colour in many cases. Blues tend to darken in colour, fawns tend to redden, creams increase their depth of colour, blacks clear to a shinier black and reds can be very deceptive. Many of the very pale red puppies become a very nice deep shade of red when older but some change to a light red instead. Some red puppies are of a lovely deep red hue when very young. There is often a faint stripe of the puppy's eventual hue in a line from the root to the tip of the tail (underneath the tail when it is carried correctly over the back).

All these breed points are referred to in greater detail in the section on the breed standard (see Chapter Five) and it is important that you familiarize yourself with this in detail so that you appreciate not only what you are looking for but why. With the exception of the minute detail, you cannot go far wrong if you look for a puppy which basically fits into squares at head, chest, body, rear and overall shape. Action is almost impossible to tell at this age but if the structure is correct there is a good chance the action will prove to be correct.

If you wish to breed or exhibit, it will be important that you study the pedigree. This collection of names may not mean much to you but the breeder should be able to explain to you not only the dogs which are winners, or producing winners, but also the reasons behind the mating of these dogs. It is not unheard of for a good winner

to come from a line not normally associated with winners. But this is a one-off chance and does not often happen. Try to start your breeding line with stock with a good breeding and showing record behind it. Even then, no cast-iron promises can be made. No-one can say more than that the puppy shows potential and promise. Unfortunately the promise is not always fulfilled. If it were that easy we would all have kennels full of Champions only!

Do not judge a puppy by its price alone. Just because a puppy is expensive does not ensure that it is healthy and well reared. Comparing prices between breeders does not mean that you are necessarily right choosing either the cheapest or the dearest. I know of one well-known and respected breeder who was told over the phone by a prospective purchaser who was just comparing prices that her puppy could not be any good because it was cheaper than another source he had investigated! You must be your

Below: *Playing with your puppy in the fresh air and sunshine will establish the essential bond between owner and puppy.*

Above: *This black puppy has silver shadings on a lovely, square bottom. The toy is a safe and sensible one.*

own judge of trust in the breeder, then listen and accept advice and finally trust your eyes and your hands.

PREPARATIONS

Although the puppy is weaned at six weeks old and technically could go to its new home then, I feel very strongly that this is too early for it to be removed from its canine family. Learning through play is a most important part of any animal's make-up and is a necessary factor in producing a psychologically balanced being. Tempting as it is to take home the little bundle of fluff you have decided upon, it is far better to leave the puppy with its littermates until it is eight to nine weeks old. You can spend those weeks profitably making sure that all is in readiness for the great day.

Where are you planning for your puppy to sleep at night? If you want it to be your bedroom then there is no harm taking it there the first night, but if not do not start it there and then expect to change it later. Wherever you choose it is essential that it is not a draughty spot. Do make sure that in any place that the puppy is likely to be left alone or asleep that there are no electrical plugs and wires which tiny teeth can gnaw. A survey will soon show that there are more of those than you thought likely and it is a very real and very serious hazard.

Is your garden area well and safely fenced? When you open your front door to callers will the puppy be able to run out on to the street? Security can be a major problem and needs much thought and probably some work before the puppy shows you just how insecure you are — possibly with disastrous or fatal results.

There are purchases to be made, and purchases not to be made. Toys are the ones which come most easily to mind. There are safe toys and unsafe ones. Beware the toys which are too soft or have odd pieces like arms, eyes, legs or tails which will be chewed off and perhaps swallowed. Beware the ball small enough to be swallowed or wedged at the back of the throat. Simple toys are often the best My puppies have great fun playing with harmless cardboard boxes, such as cereal boxes, but do make absolutely certain that you never give them any boxes with staples in them. Tights knotted many times are another favourite plaything. A log of hardwood which will not splinter can also give them hours of pleasure. You do not need to spend a fortune. Like children a puppy will often get most pleasure from inexpensive or scrap materials. The important message is that, whether bought or improvized, all toys should be checked thoroughly for complete safety.

Another would-be purchase I suggest you do not make is a dog bed. Unlike most other breeds, Chows do not seem to appreciate them. Of course there are exceptions to every rule, so I am sure that someone reading this will have a Chow which adores its bed, but most Chows seem to ignore dog beds, preferring instead an old clean blanket or a piece of synthetic fur blanket (vet-bed).

You will require a feeding bowl with a solid base and a water bowl. A suitable wire brush and a steel comb are also needed as your puppy will require a few minutes grooming every day. A collar and lead are not really required yet as the puppy will grow quite a bit before he is through his inoculation period and able to go out.

One of the most useful items you can possess is some form of play-pen. It is possible to buy purpose-made puppy pens. These are made of metal and are consequently much stronger than the wooden ones sold for children. They can also be increased in size. A child's playpen will soon become too small for a Chow puppy. My own indispensible play-pen is made of panels intended originally as an incinerator. Of course, if you are handy with tools you can easily make your own 'do-it-yourself' version. You will find so many uses for the play-pen — when the 'phone rings, when visitors come to the door, when you are cooking, when you need to leave the puppy safely for a short time, etc. But do not leave your puppy alone in it too long. It is not an easy way out for you but a safety factor for the puppy.

My other indispensible item is a metal baby-gate. This gives the puppy more freedom than the play-pen but the security of making sure the puppy stays in the area you intend him to stay in. It also stops him running up and down the stairs. Being so highly portable, it is in constant use even when the puppy has grown up.

When purchasing food for your puppy do take the breeder's advice. It is most unwise to change the food that the puppy has been used to. Even if you wish to change items or brands later, do not do this at once. Even at a later stage it must only be done gradually. You do not want a puppy with an upset tummy.

COMING HOME

You should now be ready to collect your puppy. It is important that you recheck that your puppy still appears to be healthy in all respects. Some breeders will have had the puppy recently vetted by their own veterinarian and will provide a veterinary certificate of health on purchase. Whether or not this is so, no responsible breeder will object to you having the puppy vetted at your own choice of vet, should you so wish.

Above: *Two beautiful puppies happily playing in the long grass. Note the clean dark eyes and small thick rounded ears.*

You should, before you take your puppy, make certain that you receive a receipt for the purchase money and a pedigree for your puppy. It is quite possible that the Kennel Club registration papers may not have returned by this time, but do make certain that the puppy's application for registration has already been sent to the Kennel Club. When the registration has been effected you will need to register a transfer of ownership.

You should also receive a diet sheet detailing times, amounts and content of the puppy's regular feeds. Do try to keep to this format, at least for the first week or so. It will lessen any chance of an upset stomach. Many breeders will give you a supply of the puppy's regular food to tide you over a few days and to make sure that the puppy is feeding happily.

Do check when the puppy was wormed and also what substance was used as the vermifuge. This may have been with veterinary tablets or with a very safe puppy worming fluid which is readily purchased. You may well need to continue the course of worming preparation.

Some breeders will insure the puppy for the first few weeks of its new home against loss or illness. It will then be up to you to decide whether or not you wish to continue this later. If the breeder does not do this for you, then you may think it wise to take out an insurance yourself. Accidents can happen; also puppies can very occasionally develop unexpected health problems. If you have taken the precaution of choosing a responsible breeder, they will not only wish to know of those but will certainly assist you in helping to put them right. But it is unfair to hold them responsible for the unexpected.

THE PUPPY SETTLES IN

At his new home the puppy will be finding everything very strange. He has never been on his own before without his littermates and nothing looks or smells the same. But with your love and attention he will quickly adapt. Do take care that anyone who handles him, be it family or visitor, does so with great care and sensitivity. Rough or careless handling will cause mental and physical problems he may never grow out of. Take care when picking the puppy up that the body is supported with firm hands. Never allow anyone to pick him up by the front legs. Be most careful never to drop the puppy at any time. Young children should only ever play with the puppy whilst they are on the ground. And do take great care opening and closing doors. It is only too easy to trap a puppy's feet very painfully.

Of course everyone will want to play with this little 'teddy bear' but, important as play is, it is most important that the puppy gets enough rest. Just like a growing baby, a puppy needs a lot of sleep and it is essential that he is allowed peace and quiet for this. At first he will probably need to sleep for quite long periods between meals with only a very short play period. Gradually the sleeping time will lessen until, by about six months, the puppy needs only one quiet time a day, preferably in the afternoon.

House training will probably be among the least of your problems. A Chow is normally an extremely clean animal. He does not like to soil his living area. Your puppy will probably have been trained (in fact they just about train themselves) to use newspaper as his toilet. It may be that you will need to train him that you wish him to use the garden. By putting him out as soon as he wakes up, as soon as he finishes his meal and whenever

Below: *The author with two six-week old puppies. Note the breadth of skull and the solidly boned legs with rounded paws.*

you think he might need to relieve himself, he will very quickly get the idea. It is your fault, not his, if you leave him too long. He is only a baby and when he needs to go then go he must! He will need his newspaper overnight for a few weeks but it will not be long before he is dry all night.

Feeding

There are as many feeding schedules as there are breeders and it is best for the new owner to follow the one given by their puppy's breeder. The basic outline of all schedules is much the same; it is only in details that they differ. There are two important rules to remember. Firstly, a growing puppy can only do well on the very best quality food. Never economize on cheaper varieties. Secondly, do remember that as the puppy grows so will his appetite. It is quite horrifying to hear, as some breeders have, that there has been no quantity increase on the original amount the puppy was eating when first taken home. As a guideline my own puppy diet sheet is set out below.

Additives of calcium, vitamins and minerals are important to a growing puppy. However, modern science has shown that they must not be given in excess or more harm than good will result. Modern dog foods, whether biscuit or canned, contain these additives and this must be taken into account when you feed extra. Advice given in old books was correct for those days since dog food was not as scientifically balanced as it is today. The most important time for additives to be given is during the period of most rapid growth, from six to sixteen weeks. There are good, correctly balanced all-in-one additives on the market and it is better to use that than a random mixture of tablets. Never forget that as much harm can be done by giving too much as too little.

The breeder will tell you how much the puppy is eating at the time you take him home. But he is growing fast and his appetite will increase. An increase in amount is necessary at least weekly. But your

---

Diet for a puppy

6-12 weeks
Breakfast — **4 meals a day**
Cereal or baby cereal with warm milk and glucose or lightly poached or scrambled egg with buttered wholemeal toast and a drink of milk.

Dinner
Cooked best quality butcher's mince (or minced chicken) and gravy with best quality puppy meal soaked in the gravy and fed warm. Sometimes replace the meat with cooked fish (no bones!) or grated cheese.

Tea
Rice pudding or baked egg custard or scrambled egg and milk or cereal and milk.

Supper
As dinner.

12 weeks-6 months — 3 meals a day
Breakfast, Dinner and Supper as before but leave out Tea

6 months-about 12 months — 2 meals a day
Leave out the cereal meal

12 months onwards — 1 meal a day
Your dog should now be on to one of the proprietory complete meals only having a little occasional protein addition as a tasty treat.

puppy is the best guide to how much. Chows are not greedy dogs and do not eat more than they need. Each Chow is an individual and will either cut himself down or show that he needs more. If the puppy polishes up his meal very quickly and looks for more then give him more. There was good reason for calling one of our Chows 'Oliver Twist'! I have read in a French magazine the idea that the correct amount to feed is the same amount as the size of the dog's head. A novel idea to me and one I have not put into practice, but maybe?

Never feed food straight from the fridge. Warm food is good for the puppy but make sure it is not too hot.

Clean drinking water must always be available.

Above: *Always feed puppies in separate bowls. This is soaked puppy meal and meat. A healthy puppy has a good appetite.*

Inoculations

At the age of 12 weeks it is necessary to have your puppy inoculated against hardpad, distemper, hepatitis, leptospirosis and parvovirus. Until this time, the antibodies provided by the puppy's mother have given him protection. Your veterinarian will advise you on this step. An all-in-one vaccination is usually given. You will need to take your puppy for two 'shots' and it is essential that you do not take your puppy out for walks or allow it in contact with dogs that may have been in infected areas (outdoor walks or

shows) until the vaccination course is complete.

Training
Lead training can begin at home before the puppy is ready to go out for walks. Make sure you purchase the correct type of collar and lead. The collar should be of rounded leather, not a flat one. It should fit the puppy now, not be one to grow into. Training slip collars are not a good idea for a Chow. They tangle in the coat and Chows do not react well to that kind of restraint anyway. If you really must resort to one, it must be of the rounded leather type and never a slip chain. A harness is not a good idea either since it will wear the coat and can even adversely affect the correct growth of chest and shoulders. The lead must have a very safe clip. I recommend the trigger clip as the strongest and safest. Do not try to accustom the puppy to both collar and lead at the same time. Put the collar only on the puppy. He may well not even bother about it, but if he tries to scratch it off then distract his attention with something else and he will quickly forget it. A short period of this daily, lengthening as he gets used to it and with lavish praise each time, and he will quickly accept this as routine. During this time, I train him to walk by my left side without any lead. Firstly I walk with him, speaking to him by name and keeping his attention all the time. I find that, if his attention is on you, he turns back with you and keeps beside you. This is a great game to him, played for only a very few minutes about twice daily until the

game becomes second nature to him. Only when he is good at this do I attach the lead, walking him up and down on such a loose lead that he does not object at all. The new lead has no feeling of restraint to him so he does not need to fight it. If you are not so fortunate and you do get one that objects to lead restraint, the worst thing you can do is to tug on the lead in the hope of control. You must then go with the puppy wherever he wishes until he accepts that a lead will not cause him problems. Whatever you do you must not enter into a real clash of wills. Gentle persuasion is always the answer with a Chow. You cannot praise him too much. Lessons must be kept short and enjoyable. That way you will achieve success. When he is fully inoculated and lead-trained ready to go out, do not over-walk the puppy. At first about five or ten minutes walk a day is enough. Even when a year-old, walks should not be too long or you will malform their growing bones.

Your puppy will have been trained from a very early age by the breeder to stand on a table to be groomed. You should continue this good work right from the first day you have your puppy. If he is

a very active puppy you must be very careful he does not fall. The table should be large enough to prevent this, without being so large that he thinks it is the floor! It should also have a non-slip surface and be without any wobbles. Grooming at this stage is more of a training programme than a serious necessity to groom. Through his daily few minutes (and it must not be a long session) he learns to enjoy being brushed and combed and also to submit to a daily examination of teeth, eyes and ears which is a valuable health necessity as well as being of paramount importance if he is to enter the show ring. Do use the correct flat, wire-pin brush and a good steel-toothed comb. Take great care that you never hurt the puppy by brushing too fiercely or tugging at any knots with the comb. A Chow's coat is always brushed with a finish of tail to head as the coat is a stand-off one. As with all training, the puppy should find this grooming a great pleasure and come to look forward to the

Below: *Train your puppy to walk on a loose lead. Keep watching him so that you keep in stride with each other.*

sight of the brush and comb.

Although you are doing everything you can to make your puppy's life a happy one, there will inevitably be the time when you will have to correct him. A Chow is very sensitive to correction and should be corrected with care. Never shout at your Chow. You will need a firm tone only, using a word he must come to know the meaning of — 'NO'. A light tap on his rear at the same time can assist him to know he has done wrong but it must never be a hard hit. A Chow has great respect for a folded newspaper, slapped on your own hand not on him. Given consistency both in the words you use and in when and why you use them, he will quickly learn when he has displeased you. It is most important that any reprimand is administered at the time of the offence otherwise he will not understand why you are displeased. Most important of all, forgive him quickly and let him know you still love him. Never, ever send him to bed without letting him know he is forgiven and loved.

Below: *Keep training sessions short and enjoyable. This puppy is going well and now deserves plenty of praise.*

Chapter Three

THE ADULT CHOW CHOW

FEEDING

When the Chow reaches the age of about 12 months, most owners find that it is sufficient to feed one main meal a day. Feeding time should be a regular time which fits in with your own commitments. I like to feed in the early evening, since an animal tends to settle down quietly to sleep after a meal.

In choosing the correct feed for your Chow, it is important to remember that this breed cannot be fed as much meat as most dogs. If you overdo the meat content it is highly likely that you will have a Chow with skin problems. They seem to be able to absorb protein in other forms (cheese, eggs, fish, etc) without

problems. The modern complete balanced 'all-in-one' feed with only the occasional 'taster' of meat (fresh or canned) suits most Chows. If you feed this biscuit or meal dry, do make sure it is a ready-expanded biscuit or meal otherwise the gases produced in the stomach when the dry food becomes wet could well produce the very serious problem of torsion and cause the death of your dog. With this proviso and using a quality feed from a well-established firm, the actual choice of brand lies within the taste buds of your Chow. It is good to vary the meals in taste. We would not like the same meal every day!

The amount to feed will vary from dog to dog. Like humans, some dogs get fat on very little whilst others eat a lot and stay slim. A rough guide is about 14oz (397g) a meal, but you will soon discover what the individual metabolism of your dog requires. Most Chows do not overeat but a few will.

Modern dog foods contain vitamin and mineral supplements in the correct balance. It is not advisable to add more or you could end up doing more harm than good.

It is also not advisable to give your Chow bones to gnaw. As well as causing constipation problems, I have seen cases where the gnawing action has scraped off the gum pigmentation and it has never returned. The Chows I refer to were personally known to me to have had excellent gum pigmentation before this, so it was not an owner's tale!

Clean, fresh drinking water must be available at all times.

Below Left: *Ch Treble Chance at Tanlap. A superb example of a black Chow; Top Stud Dog (Our Dogs) for 1986, 87 and 88.*

Below: *Ch Fort Knox Here's the Tiger at Towmena. Chow of the Year 1985, Top Stud Dog (Dog World) 87, Top Utility Stud 88.*

EXERCISE

The amount of exercise required depends very much on where you live. In a town situation, it is likely that you will have to walk your Chow daily, but if you live in the country with a large garden and have a couple or more Chows who can play and exercise themselves together, then walks need only be treats for their mental stimulation. It is most important that you are always in complete control of your Chow. NEVER should it be allowed out to roam on its own. Very few Chows indeed are safe to let loose off the lead. They do have a will of their own. Unless it is obedience trained (and few Chows are), your Chow should always be exercised on the lead. If your dog fouls a public area it is your responsibility to clean up the mess.

COMPANIONSHIP

Your Chow is a highly intelligent animal and he thrives on human companionship and friendship. He appreciates being talked to and treated as an equal. No matter how many you decide to own, never treat any as a caged animal in a zoo but treat each as a personal friend and member of the family. The rewards are then great for dog and man.

TRAVELLING

Most Chows love a car ride. I find that if they are started very young by travelling in the security of a travelling box with comfortable blankets, they rarely suffer from travel sickness. By the time they have grown too big for the box (about four months old), they have learned that travelling is interesting and fun. At this time they are then old enough to travel safely behind a dog guard. I clip my dogs to a controlling lead attached to the car so that they cannot jump out when a door is opened. It is a help to use window guards for ventilation. These are not sufficient to keep a car cool on a hot day. A car can quickly attain exceedingly high and dangerous temperatures on a hot day. It will become a steel torture chamber of 200°F (93°C). Brain damage occurs at 115°F (46°C). NEVER LEAVE YOUR DOG IN A PARKED CAR!

If your dog does suffer from travel sickness there are proprietary dog tablets for this. Do not use human ones since there is a fear of overdosing. Start with a low dosage gradually increasing until you find the correct amount which works. With this care, most dogs will eventually grow out of travel sickness.

Left: *Ch Chamcroft Christmas Holly. Best of Breed at Crufts 1987 and 89. Top winning puppy 86, top winning Chow 87 and 88.*

Above: *Ch Towmena Impudent Miss. An aptly-named multiple CC winner including Best of Breed at Crufts 1986.*

GROOMING

Regular grooming with the correct tools is important. You will need a slicker brush with curved, dense pins on a cushioned base and a steel-toothed comb with teeth spaced about an eighth of an inch (3mm) apart (see Chapter Five page 59). Stand your Chow on the sturdy, non-slip table he has been used to from puppyhood. First give the coat a surface brushing to remove dust, etc. If there are any tangles, be gentle. Whilst holding the coat flat with one hand, gently part the coat by brushing it in front of your hand towards the head. Go over the whole Chow, starting from the head end and working systematically towards the tail, in this manner. Remember to groom the chest and underbody gently. Pay particular attention with your comb behind the ears and under

1

Above: *With the Chow standing on a non-slip, steady table, use your slicker brush to remove surface dust.*

Below: *Pay particular attention to any tangles around the ears, parting the coat and being careful with your tools.*

2

Below: *Brushing the legs. The short leg hair needs grooming and the feathering is brushed towards the rear.*

Right: *Take care not to scratch the testicles or vulva whilst grooming the rear. Cover those parts with your free hand.*

3

4

Above: *Parting the coat carefully, the entire body is groomed right to the base. Be careful not to scratch the skin.*

Below: *Grooming the breechings. This profuse section needs your other hand to assist the careful parting of the coat.*

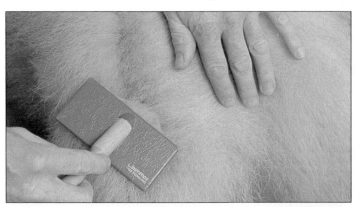

5

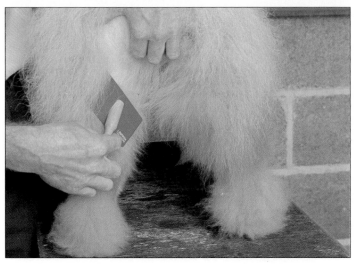

6

the forelegs, since knots will occur there unless you take care. Also use the comb for the short leg hair, remembering to comb the hocks in an upward direction. Check that ears are clean, wiping if needed gently with cotton-wool. Make sure the eyes are wiped dry. The final finish is a brushing of the coat so that it lies in a tail-to-head direction enhancing its glamour.

The breed standard of the Chow specifically states that artificial shortening of the coat is not allowed. Untidy growth of odd hairs, particularly around the mane and ears, may be lightly plucked with finger and thumb. Some Chows grow a lot of hair underneath their feet and this can be carefully trimmed back to the pads with scissors, but any other scissoring is unacceptable.

Like other dogs, the Chow will moult twice a year and will also go into a heavy moult after whelping. Being a woolly type of coat, it does not tend to stick in to furniture and clothing and is usually easily removed from these items by rolling off with a damp hand. I have

Right: *Gillian wearing a fashionable waistcoat she has knitted from the combings of her own Chows.*

also worn out many slippers by rolling it off carpets with my feet! Naturally, when the dog is moulting, grooming will need to be quite frequent. When in normal adult coat, a once-a-week groom is quite sufficient.

The woolly texture of the groomed-out hair lends itself perfectly to being hand spun. Really beautiful (and superbly warm) garments can be knitted from your Chow's cast-off coat. You can have it professionally spun or have the fun of spinning it yourself. Enquiries will usually point you to a local spinning group who will be only too happy to help you. One word of advice is

Below: *The woolly Chow coat can be spun into knitting wool. It makes the most attractive, warm and hard wearing garments.*

to learn on sheep fleece first, since dog hair does not contain as much grease and therefore is a little tricky to learn on. Also, do not keep hair for spinning from a newly-bathed Chow. There will not be sufficient natural grease in it. Do not be embarrassed that the hair is too greasy or smelly — spinners prefer it that way!

BATHING

Bathing your Chow should not be undertaken too frequently. Unless required for a special reason, it is better not to bath your Chow more often than once a year. An adult Chow's outer coat should be harsh to the touch. Too much bathing takes out the natural oils leaving it soft to the touch and floppy.

Special dog shampoos, including medicated ones, are easily obtainable. A tearless shampoo is useful. I have found that some good quality dandruff shampoos for humans are especially useful when bathing blacks.

Stand your Chow on a rubber mat in the bath to prevent slipping. Wet him all over with a warm mixer spray. Then shampoo, being very careful not to get it in his eyes or ears. Rinse thoroughly with the warm mixer spray. Wrap him in a towel and remove him to the grooming table. Blow dry thoroughly with a warm hair drier whilst combing. Be certain that he is *absolutely dry before putting him outdoors.*

Left: *The subtle shadings in this hand-knitted jacket occur naturally. Being from her own Chows, it has sentimental value.*

CARE OF THE VETERAN

The Chow is a slow maturing breed, coming to its best at around three to five years old. Many are still very active at 12 or more years old and they can live till 15 or 16. Their eyes and ears may not perceive things as sharply as of old but, in appearance, a Chow does not usually go grey round the muzzle and the coat usually stays dense and thick. An older dog will be happier with two smaller feeds a day rather than one large one and will require exercise periods to be of shorter duration at a time. Be watchful that he does not become wet, cold or chilled, since the blood circulation is now slower. As they age they seem to sleep more deeply and can become unaware that it is raining. Watch for any arthritic problems and be patient if he is slowing down. Whilst he still needs the companionship of the dogs he is used to, do not let young puppies tease him. Above all, give your veteran as much love and attention as always — more, in fact, for he has been your loved

Above: *Int Ch Chanoyu Fiery Dragon at his home in Paris. Now a veteran, he has proved to be a useful stud in France.*

Right: *Chanoyu Midnight Sirius who competed in his last show when 14 years old. He attained a record 114 Best Veteran awards.*

Below: *Edlen Commander Biggles of Brosscroft showing the vitality and love of life a veteran Chow should have.*

pet for many years and needs to know that he is still important to you. Always remember the well-known maxim: 'A DOG IS FOR LIFE, NOT FOR CHRISTMAS'.

The last farewell

Sadly, we sometimes have to make the decision to save our pet further suffering and draw its life to a peaceful end. It is never an easy decision to make but it is part of an owner's responsibility in kindness to the dog. Your veterinarian will know when the time has come and will take the decision with you. Modern drugs act quickly and painlessly. If it is at all possible, it is best for the owner to stay with the dog throughout. That way the dog has no fear and the end will be very peaceful. Distressing as this time is to the owner, if you can put your dog's needs before your own for the very short time that it takes, you will find that you can cope and help your dog at the same time. This is the very least you can do for your canine friend.

If you wish you can bury him in your own garden. There are also pet crematoria if you prefer. Most veterinarians will see that your pet is cremated for you if you wish.

THE CHOW RESCUE SERVICE

Whilst you should take on a dog for the length of its natural life, sometimes an unforeseen family crisis occurs which necessitates the Chow being found a new home. Perhaps there is a death or a divorce in the family. If, in these circumstances, you cannot find a good new home for your Chow, there exists a Chow Rescue Service which will do its best to help. You will not receive money for your Chow, but you will be able to rest assured that it will find a loving and suitable home. This service is not intended to be an easy way out for irresponsible owners but it should prevent a Chow being 'put down' in a family crisis. Also if you require a Chow, often an adult, purely as a pet with no intention of breeding from it or showing it, the Chow Rescue Service may have just what you need requiring a home.

Chapter Four

THE SMOOTH CHOW CHOW

THE smooth coated variety of Chow has a history at least as old as the rough coated variety. It is possible that it may even have been the original Chow. Certainly, when Chows were first brought into England there were as many smooths as roughs imported.

They are governed by exactly the same standard as the roughs, except for their short coat. The shorter hair should stand off the body in exactly the same way.

They have a similar dense undercoat also. The coat should look like velvet whilst still having a harsh texture. A smooth puppy's coat is short, flat and close to the skin rather like the coat on a rough adult's muzzle. The smooths lack the mane and featherings of the rough. Smooths come in the same colours as roughs but they do seem to have kept the beautiful deep self-red colour better than many roughs.

Left: *A black smooth coated Chow, Brosscroft Bolto Baer, playing in the grass with a black smooth puppy.*

Above: *Brosscroft Spun Silk showing the dignity of the smooth Chow. She is known as Jane Russell at home.*

Smooths have always had a hard time in the show ring. They have always had to compete against the roughs for top honours. Due to their coat, the true construction of the dog is there for all to see — no possibility of hiding any fault or weakness under a coat. The smooth has also kept faithfully to the original type of Chow rather than conforming to the passing fashions of heavier type, which has happened to their rough brothers. They do lose a little superficial glamour in comparison with roughs but a smooth with good conformation is a Chow of great majesty and presence.

So far there has not yet been a smooth Chow Champion in England. The first smooth to win a Challenge Certificate in England was the black bitch 'Yumsie' in 1899. Until the late 1960's, several smooth Chows were exhibited in England. Amongst many admirers of the smooths, the foremost breeders and exhibitors were Mr & Mrs Burrows who owned the 'Penhow' affix. Then came quite a long period when smooths were seen in the show ring only extremely rarely. I am pleased to say that there has been a recent revival of interest in the smooths in this country due to some devoted breeders. Smooths of quality are now being seen (and being highly placed in the show ring) much more frequently.

The largest number of smooths are to be found in Holland. This is due to the devotion of Mrs Veldhuis and of Mr & Mrs Leunissen-Rooseboom. Quality there is excellent. I speak from personal experience of judging there.

Above: *The self red Brosscroft Golden Baer has won two Reserve CC's. His light red son is Yangsing Manhattan of Brosscroft.*

Below: *Brosscroft Golden Baer, captured in relaxed mood, looking after one of his six week-old smooth puppies.*

In the US a small but devoted band of owners and breeders started the Society for the Preservation of the Smooth Chow in 1984. The first American Smooth Champion was Can & Am Ch Bearkat Little Big Man. There are now four smooth male American Champions. The first Canadian Smooth Champion was Can Ch Ciao Tiny Dancer of Foon Ying. There are also smooth Chows in France and Norway. Hopefully the band of devotees will increase in all countries where smooths are to be found.

When breeding smooth Chows, it is not possible to keep to only smooth to smooth matings due to the lack of numbers. Roughs are therefore important in maintaining the variety. Due to the necessary proximity of rough in the pedigree, even a smooth to smooth mating will often produce some roughs in the litter. There is a danger that a smooth to rough mating will produce a coat which is a little too great in length to be absolutely typical, but it is better to run this risk than lose the majestic smooth Chow. Hopefully, this recent increase in popularity will continue since it would be very sad if we lost forever this true example of the Chow.

Above: *A smooth is a very active Chow. Here, though obediently sitting, he is alert and ready for the next move.*

Above. *A smooth is a very active Chow. Here, though obediently sitting, he is alert and ready for the next move.*

Below: *Tanlap the Slicker. The true conformation of the Chow is on full display in a smooth. "And what is there to hide?" he says.*

Chapter Five

SHOWING YOUR CHOW CHOW

—— Proportions of the Chow ——

L = length; H = height
L = H
Elbow to ground = ½ H
1 = length of nose to stop
2 = length of stop to occiput
(2x1)
3 = length of neck (3x1)
6 = length of back (6x1)

Neck carriage 60 degrees

THE BREED STANDARD

A breed standard is an agreed picture in words of the ideal specimen of the breed. The first breed standard of the Chow was drawn up in 1895 by the committee of the Chow Chow Club. Since then, there have been minor clarifications culminating in the recent Kennel Club review of

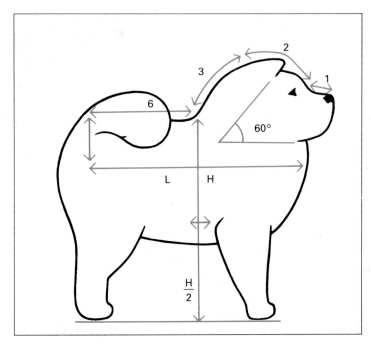

the wording of all breed standards. There has yet to be born the Chow which is an exact replica of the standard, but it is every breeder's ambition to breed as near to the ideal as possible. The standard is the ideal against which judges assess the dogs in the show-ring. Other countries have, in the main, based their standards on the English one with only very minor differences.

The overall appearance of the ideal Chow is that of a well-balanced, squarely-built animal, rather lion-like and with his tail carried proudly over his back. A Chow is a quiet dog, rarely barking and is a sensible guard dog. His loyalty is unwavering although he has a mind of his own. He is amenable to strangers in the show-ring but he is choosy about making friends.

A Chow fits roughly into squares — his head fits neatly into a square; he has a square solid front; the rear view is solid and square and the whole Chow has the perfect balance of a square.

One of the most attractive features of a Chow is his head. The strong skull is broad and flat between his thick, slightly rounded, erect ears which are carried slightly forward over the eyes. There should be enough space between those ears to fit in an imaginary 'third ear'. Interestingly, the Chow has the ability to move his ears independently rather like a horse. This results in the infuriating habit some Chows have in the ring of 'flying his ears', ie placing them awkwardly and unattractively. The correct positioning of the ears greatly assists the typical scowling expression of the Chow. This scowl (rather frightening to the uninitiated) is an expression which appears with the correct balance of facial features and not by any form of wrinkling of the skin. The eyes have a typically Eastern slant and are almond-shaped and fairly small but should not be too deep

Below: *A Chow has a strong broad flat skull; thick rounded erect ears; dark well-shaped eyes; good scowl and a moderate muzzle.*

set. The iris should be dark unless the Chow is blue or fawn when a matching iris is allowed. The muzzle is of moderate length and should remain wide throughout its length. The nose-leather is wide with good nostril space and is a solid black, although blues have a matching slate colour nose, fawns a matching darker fawn colour and creams, though starting off as puppies with a black nose, usually have an acceptable pink tinge. The strong jaws should contain regular white teeth which come together in a scissor bite. The tongue is almost unique in being a blue-black colour (any pink splashes or patches not allowable) and the flews and roof of the mouth must be black. It is preferable for the gums also to be black but puppies often take a little time to achieve this desired feature. The lips do not overhang, as in many other breeds, but meet giving a smiling expression.

To achieve the proud carriage which is desired, the Chow's strong neck should be of reasonable length and set on to his sloping, muscular shoulders at an angle of approximately 60 degrees. His straight front legs should have good strong bone right down to his small, rounded, cat-like feet. He should stand up well on his toes, never being flat-footed. His chest and rib-cage should be broad and deep giving plenty of heart room and the rib-cage should extend well back along the body to give plenty of room for the lungs. The desired cobby, short back should never be achieved by a short rib-cage but be due to the shortness of coupling between the end of the rib-cage and the haunch. The spine must be both straight and level. The well-boned hind legs have little angulation, the rear foot being in perpendicular line with the hip and the hocks set low. This gives the Chow the short, stilted action which is so characteristic of the breed. It is most interesting to see a Chow's tracks in the snow. Instead of four paw marks you will see the two front paw marks but

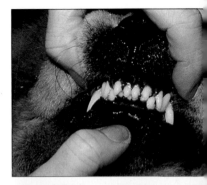

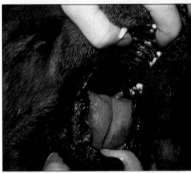

Top: *The Chow should have a scissor bite. The gums are preferably black and the lips and flews black.*

Above: *A Chow's tongue is bluish black and the roof of the mouth is black. A good mouth is rather like a 'coal-hole'!*

the hind marks are two oblongs where the hock has thrown the snow off. Perhaps the stilted action was a necessary evolution in the snowy wasteland of his ancestors. In movement both fore and aft, the legs should move parallel to each other showing daylight between them. At all times the high-set tail should be carried well and tightly over the back. A male Chow should be 'entire', that is he should have both testicles descended into the scrotum.

There are two kinds of coat — the more usual rough and the rarer smooth. They differ only in length of outer hair. Both must be straight,

Above: *This bitch is showing an ideally arched neck, correctly placed beautifully shaped ears and a clean well-shaped eye.*

Below: *A Chow should stand four square on strong, straight legs. The chest should have a hand's breadth between the legs.*

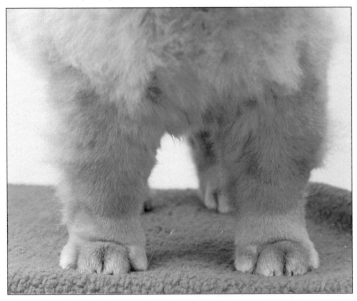

Above: *The bright self-red is one of the most attractive colourings. Many self-reds have a shorter stand-off coat.*

Right: *Miminic Misty Dawn is a good example of the elusive colour fawn. Fawns can vary from very pale to deep cinnamon.*

thick and dense and both must stand off well from the body with a good undercoat. The quality of both adult coats must be harsh to the touch. The rough variety will have a good mane and fairly profuse trousers. It is definitely not allowable to trim the coat with scissors to alter the shape and apparent balance. The Chow varies greatly in colour. The most usual is red, either as a solid colour or with lighter shadings on the trousers and tail. Becoming much more usual of recent years is the black, again either solid colour or with silver shadings on trousers and tail. The more unusual Chow colours are blue (a slatey grey like the colour of a blue Persian cat), fawn (a silvery haze over brown) and cream (an attractive creamy colour with apricot coloured ears).

The new English standard now gives a more detailed size limitation. Adult bitches should measure 18-20in (46-51cm) at the shoulder and adult dogs 19-22in (48-56cm). Puppies will still be growing and should not be expected to have reached full height. They are not necessarily fully grown until approximately 18 months old for a Chow is a slow developer. In Europe the FCI standard was based on the English one. They have had a height standard of 46cm (18in) for some years. The American standard, though worded slightly differently from the English, has the same intentions as the English standard but their height standard is 17-20in (43-51cm). The Canadians have adopted the American standard.

I have given an outline of the meaning of the standard. The actual breed standard can be obtained through Breed Clubs or direct from the Kennel Club.

Above: *A cream has an apricot tinge to his coat and attractive apricot ears. Good pigment can be found if correctly bred.*

Below: *A blue is a smokey grey. It can have silver shadings, as here, or be a solid colour. Notice the matching slate nose.*

THE SHOW RING

Entering your Chow in shows can bring a new and absorbing interest in your life. Your Chow will not match up to the Standard in all respects — the perfect dog has yet to be born. If you attend some shows before you decide to exhibit you will have some idea as to whether or not your Chow is likely to be of show quality. Also the breeder of your dog will be only too pleased to advise you. Attendance at some shows will also assist you to see just what showing your dog entails. Maybe you will be very fortunate at your first show and do some good winning, or maybe it will not be your dog's lucky day. Whichever it is, be prepared to accept your wins or losses gracefully. There is always another day, another judge.

Training for the show ring

In the show ring your Chow will be expected to be handled by a stranger (the judge), to stand four-square and reasonably still, and to show his action by moving in a controlled way. The good habits of mouth, eye and ear inspection you have instilled in your Chow at grooming sessions will pay dividends. Friends, neighbours and welcome visitors should all have been encouraged to handle your Chow with gentleness and lavish praise. Your Chow is now used to walking beside you on a loose lead. Now all that remains is for you to learn what is expected of an exhibitor in the ring and to get your dog used to the atmosphere of a show. The best place to do this is at a local ring-training class. Most areas run evening classes at which the ringcraft skills may be learned by both dog and owner. These are great fun and good social occasions. Here your dog will get used to mixing with others, being handled for show-ring examination by strangers and moving at the correct speed.

Your dog's stance is most important for it creates both the judge's first and last impression of the dog. He must stand with his

Above right: *A perfect show position showing an alert, squarely built dog. The handler is shading her dog on a hot day.*

Below: *A selection of suitable collars, slips and leads. Notice the strong trigger clips on the leads.*

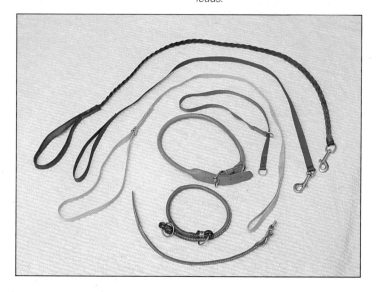

dog in his stride walking round you whilst you turn on the spot) and return to the judge. At all times keep your dog on a loose lead. A tight lead will affect your dog's movement to his disadvantage.

Making your entries

When entering your dog for his first show, do not make the mistake of entering too many classes. Both of you are beginners and both need to learn slowly. Do study the definitions of classes and choose suitable classes. If you need any assistance deciding on classes, ask your dog's breeder or the show secretary.

Getting ready for show day

Before the show, do give some thought as to what to wear. Dress to complement your dog, not to dominate the picture your dog presents. For example, it does your dog no favours if you exhibit a black dog against a black skirt or black trousers. The rule to remember is that a dark dog silhouettes against a light background and vice versa.

Your dog will need the following equipment: brush, comb, water bowl and bottle of water, towel, tissues, a blanket to lie on either on the floor or on the bench. If it is a

feet four-square, using his neck carriage to his advantage and with his tail held tightly on his back.

When the judge feels over your dog for construction it is a good idea to give your dog confidence by holding or stroking him.

When told to move your dog in a triangle, walk away from the judge, with your dog at your left side, to a point in the far right hand corner of the ring, turn to your left and walk straight ahead to the left-hand corner, turn to your left again and walk in a straight line back to the judge. When asked to move up and down, walk directly away from the judge, at the end of the ring turn to your right (this keeps the

Below: *A selection of suitable grooming items: steel-toothed combs and slicker brushes with cushion-based pins.*

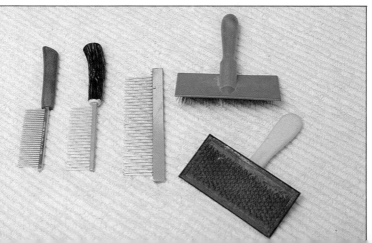

benched show, you will need a benching chain (you can purchase these at shows). I find a gas-filled hair styling brush useful to dry up a dribbly chin effectively. If you have a suitable grooming table, it is helpful to take it.

Do not forget to take your show pass, if one is sent, and your schedule. British exhibitors will need a ring clip with which to anchor your ring number. These are obtainable very cheaply at shows.

At the show

Arrive at the show in good time to settle both yourself and your dog calmly and to have time for final grooming before entering the ring. Try not to be nervous. Nerves transmit themselves straight down the lead to the dog and will result in your dog losing all his confidence. Keep your mind on your dog rather than on yourself and nerves will disappear.

When your class is called by the ring steward, collect your ring number and pin it on (or in the USA and Canada, wear your armband on the left arm) and take your dog into the line at the side of the ring and stand your dog up ready for the judge's inspection. After your dog has been individually examined, return to the line and praise your dog. After the last dog has been examined, stand your dog up again whilst the judge makes his final decision. If you are selected as a winner you will be placed in order in the centre of the ring, ready to receive your prize card or ribbon. Whether you win or lose, accept the decision with grace. Another day the placings may be totally different.

Below: *Keep your dog in the shade on a hot day while waiting for his class. The towel is mopping up any dribbles.*

Above: *A class of Chows at a Summer Breed Open show in England, with a cricket match in the background!*

Enjoy the rest of the day with your new-found friends. Win or lose, you will probably leave the show with plans for entering the next one. If so then, like so many of us, the 'show bug' will have got you and you will have become one of the band of friends who are enthusiastic Chowists.

THE BRITISH SHOW SYSTEM

In Britain, shows are held under the regulations set by the Kennel Club. There are various grades of shows. Breed shows are ones held for one particular breed of dog. Variety shows are for all breeds and may or may not have some classes just for your own breed. Whatever type of show it is, a puppy cannot be entered until it is six months of age.

Exemption shows
These are local, friendly events held in aid of charity. They are licensed by the Kennel Club but have much freer rules than any other shows. They can accept dogs which are not registered, both pedigree and non-pedigree. Entries can be made on the day. Basically they are fun events but they are very useful training grounds for trying out the show world.

Sanction shows
These are small shows, usually variety shows. Dogs which have won high honours in the show ring are not allowed to compete at these shows.

Limited shows
These are limited to members of the Society (membership is inexpensive) and can be variety shows or breed shows. Dogs which have won awards which count towards the title of Champion are not allowed to be entered.

Open shows
These shows are open to all dogs whether Champions or not.

Championship shows
These are open to all. It is only at these shows that Challenge Certificates (known as CCs) are awarded. It takes 3 CCs won under three different judges for a dog to be awarded the coveted title of

Champion. One of the CCs at least must be won when the dog is over 12 months old.

Crufts Dog Show

Crufts is the only show for which a dog has to qualify before it can be entered. Qualifications vary very slightly from year to year. Champions, winners of CCs and Reserve CCs, dogs entered in the Stud Book by virtue of their wins in top classes at Championship shows, and first prize winners of certain classes at Championship shows are eligible for entry at this prestige event.

Above: *A group of exhibitors enjoying a relaxing chat under a cooling Chow umbrella — naturally talking about Chows!*

THE CONTINENTAL SHOW SYSTEM

In Europe, all dog shows are governed by regulations laid down by the FCI (Federation Cynologique Internationale). Each country also has its own Kennel Club. There are two kinds of show, Championship shows and small fun shows usually held by breed clubs. There are

many fewer shows on the Continent than there are in Britain.

Judging takes the form of grading into excellent, very good, good or sufficient and a written critique is given on each exhibit at the time of judging. This can make the judging procedure a very lengthy one. Dogs can usually only be entered in one class at a time.

Only those dogs awarded an Excellent can be awarded a Best of Sex award. If the Best of Sex is considered to be worthy, it may be awarded the CAC (Certificat d'Aptitude au Championat) or, if it is an International Show, the CACIB (Certificat d'Aptitude au Championat International de Beauté). To become a Champion, a dog must be awarded 3 CAC or CACIB under two different judges with at least a 12-month interval between first and last certificates. These certificates may be won in any country affiliated to the FCI. There are also individual regulations regarding the awarding of each country's Championship title and also to the award of the title of International Champion.

Below: *The top winners line up with the judge. From left to right: Reserve Best in Show, Best Bitch, BIS and Best Puppy.*

THE NORTH AMERICAN SYSTEM

In America and Canada, the Breed shows are called Speciality Shows. There are several classes with definitions according to age, show wins or country of origin. As in Britain, you cannot show a dog until it is six months old. The first prize winners compete for the title of Winners Dog and Winners Bitch. Only Winners Dog and Winners Bitch may be awarded Championship points. The Winners then go on to challenge the first prize winners of the Champions class for Best of Breed.

There are also All-Breed shows which run on the same lines but cater for many breeds at the same show. As in Britain, the Best of Breed winners will go on to compete for Best in Group and the Group Winners for Best in Show.

To become a Champion, the dog must gain 15 points under at least three different judges. The number of points awarded at each show varies with the geographical location and the number of dogs entered. Each Champion must have won at least two major points shows under different judges. The major points shows will award a minimum of three points, but no

show may award more than five points.

There are also sanctioned matches for pedigree dogs held by both all-breed and breed clubs. No Championship points are awarded. These are an excellent opportunity for learning more about every aspect of showing. Sometimes they will run special classes at a puppy match for puppies of three to 12 months of age.

JUDGING

Although different countries have different methods of appointing judges, they all start with the most important criteria for a judge — experience and in-depth knowledge of the breed. The various Kennel Clubs have different requirements as to the length of time required as experience. This is probably due to the fact that both Chows and dog shows are more numerous in some countries than others. In both the USA and Canada, judges are licensed by their respective Kennel Clubs. In the USA, Canada and in France, prospective judges are set tests to show their knowledge of the breed. Training of judges in France includes some attendance at a Veterinary College in order to understand the basic structure of the dog. The British method has, until recent years, relied solely upon a reputation for breeding and exhibiting dogs of quality for a person to have their name added to a Breed Club's judging list for smaller shows. By progression of the amount of judging experience, the judge progresses upwards to larger shows other than Championship shows. Eventually the judge's track record of showing, breeding and judging is considered by the Show Committee of the Kennel Club for KC approval as a Championship show judge. Of recent years, various training schemes for prospective judges have been started, both for variety judges and for breed specialists. Although this is not a Kennel Club requirement,

the Kennel Club looks favourably upon education for judges. I certainly wish something like this had been around when I first started rather than learning 'on the job'! At the time of writing, six of the British Breed Clubs for Chows have a system of education plus assessment as the requirement for being placed on their respective judging lists.

Preparation for judging
After serving a good apprenticeship in breeding and exhibiting your Chows and, hopefully, having attended the education lectures and passed the assessment, and with your judging appointment now very close, you will need to prepare for your appearance in the centre of the

Above: *The judge watches an exhibit move. The exhibitor tries to return the Chow to moving in a straight line.*

ring. Always re-read the breed standard the night before judging. Never become too blasé to do this, since it will put back into perspective the overall balanced picture you should be looking for. Although many judges now dictate their comments on the exhibits into a small tape recorder, I have a distrust of these machines. Even if you make no errors pressing the right buttons, it is only too easy to make such similar remarks about the exhibits that, upon playing it back, no clear picture exists to differentiate one dog from another.

Personally I prefer to use a note-book ruled under headings of the breed standard. This I prepare before the show. Find a little 'something' which will make an interesting sound for a dog. This will help to get the dog which is 'flying his ears' to show his correct ear placement. A small match-box with a few buttons or other rattly objects is ideal.

Whilst wearing something comfortable, do make sure that it is neither too bright nor too vividly patterned. Colours may not be perceived by dogs in the same way as we see them but they do react to colour. Keep all clothing under control so that it does not flap over the dog's face. Do not wear perfume or aftershave — dogs have an acute sense of smell.

On the day

Be on time and report to the secretary early. Make a thorough assessment of your ring to see which way will be best for assessing movement, where the lighting will help you best to judge eye colour, where there is shade on a hot day, etc. Always make the best use of your ring in order to get the best out of the exhibits.

When the first class enters, do not be in a hurry to rush into assessment. Take your time and walk calmly up and down the line getting the initial picture of the dogs into your mind. This will calm any 'first night nerves' you may have. When judging classes of younger dogs and puppies, it often helps them to settle if you send them to walk before you handle them. A Chow likes to make the first approach so I find that they handle more readily if the owner is asked to bring the dog from the walk straight up to me, rather than have me approach the dog. Look and feel for construction and movement. Remember to check gently that both testicles are descended in a male. Be firm but gentle with your hands and you will instill confidence into the dog. The exhibitor is trying to get the best out of his or her dog and will appreciate your efforts to do the same for his dog. Always believe what your hands tell you — your eyes can be deceived! Look for positive, good points and do not fall into the trap of judging by faults alone. Be methodical in your manner of assessment and you will not then miss anything. Before placing in order, try to regain an overall positive picture of the exhibit against the standard. Look for the proud carriage, the arrogance and the character of the Chow. Then place your winners.

The critique

On the Continent, you will be expected to write a critique on every dog exhibited. This is done at the time of judging and is handed to the exhibitor at the show. In England, a critique is written on the first and second placements at Championship shows and on first placements only at other shows. These are published in the Dog Press.

Below: *The judge feels under the coat for correct conformation. Here she is checking shoulder placement.*

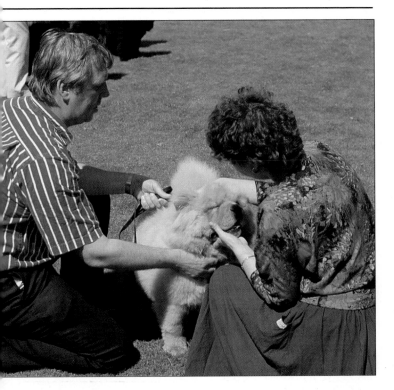

Records

It is most important that you keep accurate records of dates, places, numbers of classes and numbers of dogs judged. It is also important that you keep records of show wins of dogs both owned by you and also of dogs owned by others but bred by you. This information is required by the Kennel Club for reference when appointing Championship show judges in Britain and it may well be required by kennel clubs in other countries for judging appointments. It is essential that this information is accurate.

OBEDIENCE SHOWS

It is unlikely that your Chow will ever attain the standard of perfection necessary to compete in Obedience shows. A Chow will never attain the slick, speedy, submissive obedience of the Border Collie. But this need not prevent you from attending fun

Above: *It is important to check eyes for colour, shape and lack of entropion. Check, as here, by looking, not by pulling about.*

shows and giving exhibitions if you and your Chow feel so inclined. In England I have known very few Chows to perform show obedience work. Interestingly they have all been black and a study of their pedigrees reveals a common ancestry.

It takes time, patience and concentrated effort on the part of Chow and owner. Sits, stays and recalls can all, given patience, be achieved and performed without fault. But Chows seem to find the retrieve rather alien to their nature. Most have the idea of 'you threw it, you fetch it!'. Unlike many other breeds, once out of puppyhood, few Chows find chasing a ball or fetching a stick of any interest. Some Chows will learn to retrieve but then have little sympathy with having to 'hold' it until a command to take is ordered. Scenting, too, seems to be alien to the nature of most Chows.

If you intend to obedience train your Chow, the following tips may help. Retrieving is 'work' not a game, so puppy play with a ball should not be encouraged unless as part of training. Never use a choke chain on your Chow. Not only will it ruin his mane but he will resent its use. If you must use a controlling slip (and most Chows are better controlled on a collar), then it must be of the rolled leather type. Always have different types of collar and lead for obedience and for show. Your Chow will soon learn to associate them with the style of work you are expecting him to perform.

Normally obedient behaviour, as opposed to the extra demands of show obedience work, should definitely be taught. You need to have a dog which comes when called and will stay on command, particularly for safety in the car.

If you have the inclination, inordinate patience and the time plus a suitably-minded Chow, then great fun can be had at the lower level of Obedience competition.

But the Chow will never become the precise automaton required in present-day top competition. Your reward will be that you have a socialized animal.

Left: *Chris is putting Zak into his 'sitting at heel' position by the use of a 'see-saw' movement of her hands.*

Above: *Zak is left in 'wait' position before being called to heel. Note the long lead used in training.*

Below left: *The finished exercise with Zak in heel position, waiting for his well-deserved praise.*

Below: *Most Chows are not keen on retrieving. Here, Zak seems to be saying, "Will this do today, Mum?"*

Chapter Six

BREEDING YOUR CHOW CHOW

A BREEDER'S RESPONSIBILITIES

Breeding puppies brings with it responsibilities. It is important that you think very seriously about your reasons for breeding. It is very definitely not a 'get rich quick' pastime. Neither is it 'good for the bitch' to have puppies. Your aim must be to produce sound, healthy, quality puppies with excellent temperaments.

You will need to consider whether you have the time to spare, the space to devote and the money to raise them well. There is not much profit in rearing puppies if you do the job properly. The pregnant bitch will require extra food of high quality. By the time the puppies are sold at eight weeks, they will have been consuming four meals a day for a long while. Their mother will also have finished with keeping them clean and dry so you will be forever cleaning up their toilet newspapers. You should also be certain of finding the right homes for the puppies before you consider breeding with your bitch.

If you are to breed healthy, quality puppies it is important that your bitch is a good specimen of the breed and that she has a perfect temperament. If you buy a bitch as a pet that is how she should remain. She should not be used as a brood bitch.

You should be able to advise prospective buyers on all aspects of rearing and training the puppies and should be prepared to be on hand if they need help — even to the extent of helping if the puppy unexpectedly needs rehoming in the future.

Much forward thought and planning is essential before deciding to breed with your bitch. Always remember that you are responsible for bringing that puppy into the world and your responsibilities to that puppy remain there for the whole of that puppy's life.

CHOOSING THE STUD DOG

Do not be tempted into using the nearest male dog. Study the available stud dogs for their temperament, their conformation and what they are producing. Study, too, the pedigrees of both any intended stud dog and your bitch. Discuss your plans with knowledgeable breeders. Take the advice of the breeder of your bitch who will have the experience of what should be the right mating for that line.

Know your own bitch's faults and virtues. Try to double up on her virtues and correct her faults by choosing a male strong in those features. Enquire about the family of the stud dog for several generations to acquire this information. Do not mate two together with the same hereditary faults. Although entropion (see Chapter Seven) is surgically correctable, it will still be passed on. Other important hereditary faults to consider are hip dysplasia and breathing problems. You neither do the breed nor yourselves any favour by perpetuating these painful conditions.

If it is your bitch's first litter, it is unwise to choose an unproven dog. If no litter ensues the fault could lie with either.

Choose your stud dog well in advance before your bitch comes

Below: *Lechan Moonlighting. Top Chow puppy (*Our Dogs*)1988 and Junior Warrant. A good example of careful line breeding.*

into season and be prepared to travel a fair distance if need be (on what will probably prove to be a most inconvenient date to yourself) to mate your bitch to a sound, healthy, typically representative specimen of the breed with a compatible pedigree.

MATCHING PEDIGREES

There are three different ways of matching the pedigrees of the bitch and the stud. They are technically called in-breeding, line breeding and outcrossing.

In-breeding
This is the mating of very closely related dogs, eg father to daughter, brother to sister, etc. This method can fix desirable qualities but it also doubles up very strongly on any undesirable features and any recessive genetics. In the hands of the expert it can produce excellent stock (and it has). But it is far too dangerous for the novice to experiment with and is not to be recommended.

Line breeding
This is the careful selection of the best dogs in a line and breeding back to them. It is the mating of related animals two or three generations removed, eg great grandson to granddaughter, grand-daughter to grandson, etc. This, too, doubles the bad points as well as the good but to a lesser degree. It is most important that you know what you are doing and why. Only line breed to dogs which are physically and temperamentally sound. Line bred puppies have a greater chance of inheriting their forebears characteristics. Most successful kennels breed on these lines, since they can keep to a uniform and established type. Line breeding needs the expert advice of your bitch's breeder but should prove to be a successful avenue to pursue.

Below: *Ch Suntory Mimosa. Winner of Chow of the Year in 1987. Notice the correctly placed feet and the alert expression.*

Outcrossing

This is the mating of unrelated dogs. This course is usually taken to improve a specific physical or temperamental point. It is also used when line breeding has been pursued for several generations to the point where the progeny is becoming too in-bred so that an unrelated outcross is required. As long as you do not use a dog with the same fault(s) as your bitch, outcrossing can be useful but it produces less uniform results than line breeding.

MATING

A bitch usually comes into season first at about six months old and thereafter every six months. Every bitch has her individual pattern however, so it is important to discover your own bitch's natural rhythm. A bitch should be allowed to mature before mating. Ideally she should be mated on the season which is nearest to the time when she is 18 months old. Thereafter it is best to allow her to be mated only on alternate seasons so that she has time to fully recover herself. It is important that she is in peak condition at the time of mating. If she is too fat, the chances of conception are reduced. As soon as she comes in season book your stud dog.

The normal oestrus (season) lasts for three weeks. For the first ten days there is a bright red discharge from the vulva which gradually fades to pale pink. The normal time for mating is from the 10th to 16th day, but all bitches are individual and some are ready earlier, some later. A good sign that she is ready is when the colour has paled off and the vulva is obviously swollen. She may also be curling her tail to one side when you place your hand on her back. But the one who really knows whether or not it is the right time is the experienced stud dog.

Chows are not the easiest dogs to mate. Chow bitches are known as 'good mothers but lousy mistresses'! It is a rare Chow.

which mates without assistance. Most need strong hands controlling the bitch on a strong collar. Some bitches panic and, unless held firmly, could damage either themselves or the stud dog. It is helpful to use your knees to control the bitch's shoulders if needed. Follow the instructions of the stud dog's owner, since they know their own dog's likes and dislikes. They do not want their stud dog injured.

Most dogs will 'tie' with their bitch. That is when the dog's penis has entered the bitch's vulva it will swell, so preventing them separating until it returns to normal size. During this time it is customary for the mating pair to turn back to back. This is a much more comfortable position for all concerned, including the human handlers! The 'tie' can last anything from five to 45 minutes. It is not, however, essential to producing puppies. Many litters are born from matings without a 'tie'. It is in the first few minutes of ejaculation that the sperm enters the bitch. During the 'tie' it is most important to keep control of both the dogs since it is then that serious damage can ensue if one or other (usually the bitch) panics.

It is best to have two matings 48 hours apart. The gradual ovulation process within the bitch is of uncertain timing. The sperm remains active within the bitch for 24 hours. By mating twice with one rest day between you cover 48 hours of possible ovulation time.

The stud fee is payable at the time of mating. The fee is a payment for the service whether or not there is a resultant litter. Most breeders, however, will give a free return mating on the next season if no litter has resulted. This arrangement must be made clear, and should be put in writing, at the time of this initial mating. You should have a receipt for your fee. You will also need to be certain that you are given the green Kennel Club form for registration of the litter with the signed state-ment of mating on it. This you will complete when the litter is born.

THE LADY-IN-WAITING

You now have about 63 days to wait till whelping day. But be prepared; some Chow bitches tend to whelp a few days early. For the first four or five weeks you will be kept wondering, for there will be little sign of pregnancy. Any sign there is will be likely to be temperamental rather than physical. She may become calmer and more affectionate than usual. Some bitches show a colourless discharge from the vulva when pregnant but, unless this becomes of an offensive nature, there is no need to worry.

Supplementary feeding can begin about the fifth week. You do not need to feed extra carbohydrates, since you are not encouraging her to become fat. At this time she needs the extra protein of meat, fish, eggs or cheese and also extra vitamin and mineral supplements (including a calcium supplement) in the form of a balanced additive. Great demands are being placed on her body reserves at this time. Her normal feed should be split into two smaller helpings so that it does not lay heavy on her stomach. She also needs an extra meal of cereal, milk and egg.

It is important that she continues to exercise. But, as her burden increases, make sure that this exercise is short and frequent and let her dictate the pace. Do not let her jump up.

During the final two weeks of waiting, the coat will start to come off her tummy. Gently remove it for

Right: *Cedar is heavy in whelp with only 12 more days to wait. Gentle exercise, frequent small meals and no jumping at this time.*

Gestation table

Jan	Mar	Feb	Apr	Mar	May	Apr	June	May	Jul	Jun	Aug
1 due 4		1 due 4		1 due 2		1 due 2		1 due 2		1 due 2	
2 due 5		2 due 5		2 due 3		2 due 3		2 due 3		2 due 3	
3 due 6		3 due 6		3 due 4		3 due 4		3 due 4		3 due 4	
4 due 7		4 due 7		4 due 5		4 due 5		4 due 5		4 due 5	
5 due 8		5 due 8		5 due 6		5 due 6		5 due 6		5 due 6	
6 due 9		6 due 9		6 due 7		6 due 7		6 due 7		6 due 7	
7 due 10		7 due 10		7 due 8		7 due 8		7 due 8		7 due 8	
8 due 11		8 due 11		8 due 9		8 due 9		8 due 9		8 due 9	
9 due 12		9 due 12		9 due 10		9 due 10		9 due 10		9 due 10	
10 due 13		10 due 13		10 due 11		10 due 11		10 due 11		10 due 11	
11 due 14		11 due 14		11 due 12		11 due 12		11 due 12		11 due 12	
12 due 15		12 due 15		12 due 13		12 due 13		12 due 13		12 due 13	
13 due 16		13 due 16		13 due 14		13 due 14		13 due 14		13 due 14	
14 due 17		14 due 17		14 due 15		14 due 15		14 due 15		14 due 15	
15 due 18		15 due 18		15 due 16		15 due 16		15 due 16		15 due 16	
16 due 19		16 due 19		16 due 17		16 due 17		16 due 17		16 due 17	
17 due 20		17 due 20		17 due 18		17 due 18		17 due 18		17 due 18	
18 due 21		18 due 21		18 due 19		18 due 19		18 due 19		18 due 19	
19 due 22		19 due 22		19 due 20		19 due 20		19 due 20		19 due 20	
20 due 23		20 due 23		20 due 21		20 due 21		20 due 21		20 due 21	
21 due 24		21 due 24		21 due 22		21 due 22		21 due 22		21 due 22	
22 due 25		22 due 25		22 due 23		22 due 23		22 due 23		22 due 23	
23 due 26		23 due 26		23 due 24		23 due 24		23 due 24		23 due 24	
24 due 27		24 due 27		24 due 25		24 due 25		24 due 25		24 due 25	
25 due 28		25 due 28		25 due 26		25 due 26		25 due 26		25 due 26	
26 due 29		26 due 29		26 due 27		26 due 27		26 due 27		26 due 27	
27 due 30		27 due 30		27 due 28		27 due 28		27 due 28		27 due 28	
28 due 31		28 due 1 May		28 due 29		28 due 29		28 due 29		28 due 29	
29 due 1 Apr				29 due 30		29 due 30		29 due 30		29 due 30	
30 due 2 Apr				30 due 31		30 due 1 July		30 due 31		30 due 31	
31 due 3 Apr				31 due 1 Jun				31 due 1 Aug			

Table based on 63 days inclusive of both dates, leap years not allowed for.

Jul	Sept	Aug	Oct	Sept	Nov	Oct	Dec	Nov	Jan	Dec	Feb
1 due 1		1 due 2		1 due 2		1 due 2		1 due 2		1 due 1	
2 due 2		2 due 3		2 due 3		2 due 3		2 due 3		2 due 2	
3 due 3		3 due 4		3 due 4		3 due 4		3 due 4		3 due 3	
4 due 4		4 due 5		4 due 5		4 due 5		4 due 5		4 due 4	
5 due 5		5 due 6		5 due 6		5 due 6		5 due 6		5 due 5	
6 due 6		6 due 7		6 due 7		6 due 7		6 due 7		6 due 6	
7 due 7		7 due 8		7 due 8		7 due 8		7 due 8		7 due 7	
8 due 8		8 due 9		8 due 9		8 due 9		8 due 9		8 due 8	
9 due 9		9 due 10		9 due 10		9 due 10		9 due 10		9 due 9	
10 due 10		10 due 11		10 due 11		10 due 11		10 due 11		10 due 10	
11 due 11		11 due 12		11 due 12		11 due 12		11 due 12		11 due 11	
12 due 12		12 due 13		12 due 13		12 due 13		12 due 13		12 due 12	
13 due 13		13 due 14		13 due 14		13 due 14		13 due 14		13 due 13	
14 due 14		14 due 15		14 due 15		14 due 15		14 due 15		14 due 14	
15 due 15		15 due 16		15 due 16		15 due 16		15 due 16		15 due 15	
16 due 16		16 due 17		16 due 17		16 due 17		16 due 17		16 due 16	
17 due 17		17 due 18		17 due 18		17 due 18		17 due 18		17 due 17	
18 due 18		18 due 19		18 due 19		18 due 19		18 due 19		18 due 18	
19 due 19		19 due 20		19 due 20		19 due 20		19 due 20		19 due 19	
20 due 20		20 due 21		20 due 21		20 due 21		20 due 21		20 due 20	
21 due 21		21 due 22		21 due 22		21 due 22		21 due 22		21 due 21	
22 due 22		22 due 23		22 due 23		22 due 23		22 due 23		22 due 22	
23 due 23		23 due 24		23 due 24		23 due 24		23 due 24		23 due 23	
24 due 24		24 due 25		24 due 25		24 due 25		24 due 25		24 due 24	
25 due 25		25 due 26		25 due 26		25 due 26		25 due 26		25 due 25	
26 due 26		26 due 27		26 due 27		26 due 27		26 due 27		26 due 26	
27 due 27		27 due 28		27 due 28		27 due 28		27 due 28		27 due 27	
28 due 28		28 due 29		28 due 29		28 due 29		28 due 29		28 due 28	
29 due 29		29 due 30		29 due 30		29 due 30		29 due 30		29 due 1 Mar	
30 due 30		30 due 31		30 due 1 Dec		30 due 31		30 due 31		30 due 2 Mar	
31 due 1 Oct		31 due 1 Nov				31 due 1 Jan				31 due 3 Mar	

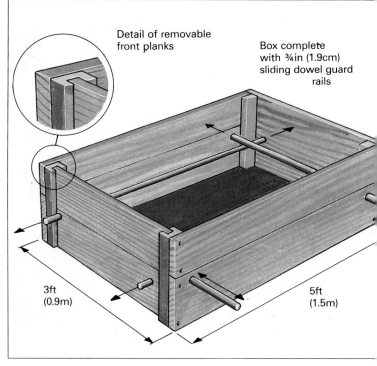

Detail of removable front planks

Box complete with ¾in (1.9cm) sliding dowel guard rails

3ft (0.9m)

5ft (1.5m)

Above: *An easily constructed whelping box which will stack in sections when not in use. The dowel rods are also removable.*

you do not want sucking puppies to swallow fur. Also, during those last two weeks, introduce her to her whelping quarters.

THE WHELPING QUARTERS

It is vital that the whelping quarters are warm with no draughts. They should also be a quiet area away from human family and other dogs. Whilst it is possible to have good outdoor kennels for whelping, I prefer to set aside a spare room in the house. This is far more convenient for keeping the watchful eye you will need to have.

The wooden whelping box itself can be made very easily with little practical knowledge of carpentry. Having lost puppies in the past by suffocation in a 3ft (91cm) square box, I have come to the conclusion that a much larger box is better. My present box is approximately 5ft by 3ft (1.5 x 0.9m). It gives plenty of room for the bitch to opt either to lie close to her puppies or

slightly apart from them. It is made of flooring planks, two planks high with a removable front. Inside there is a guard rail on all four sides about 5ins (13cm) up from the base. This prevents a puppy being accidentally lost and smothered behind the bitch. The whole box takes apart for storage using only a few screws. The base is three sections of strawboard-type flooring, also easy to store.

During the actual whelping, the box is lined with plenty of newspapers. The bitch will scratch these up during whelping. They are easily changed as they become shredded and dirty. Later, when whelping is complete, I substitute synthetic fur (veterinary) bedding which is warm, comfortable and easy to wash. You will need to be

Above: *An ingenious whelping box and pen which can partition the pups into a warm area with the infra-red height very variable.*

Below: *The same whelping box opened out for the older litter with a carpeted slope now let down for easy access to the pen.*

watchful of this in case your bitch scratches this up, even though it is anchored down, since you do not want your puppies to be accidentally suffocated.

Above the box I suspend an infra-red lamp at a height of approximately 5ft (1.5m). This gives the gentle, constant warmth necessary for the new-born pups without frying them or their mother. It also gives sufficient gentle light at night-time. I firmly believe that the infra-red helps to dry out any little lungs from any retained mucous.

Plenty of warm, rough towels will be needed to dry off the puppies. A pair of scissors in a jar of disinfectant and water and some white button thread should be ready in case you need to tie and sever the umbilical cords. A box with a covered hot water bottle is useful to put the first puppies in whilst another puppy is arriving (though you may not always use it). Lastly, have a notebook and pencil ready, plus a clock, so that you can note down the progress of the whelping. This can be useful for reference on her subsequent whelpings and, if anything goes wrong and you have to call your veterinarian, the information there will be invaluable.

WHELPING

Well before the projected date of whelping it is advisable to inform your veterinarian that your bitch is expecting a litter.

Chows are average whelpers. They vary temperamentally in behaviour at this time. There are three stages of labour. Some Chows will have a very lengthy first stage, others a very short one. The first stage of labour is characterized by behavioural disturbances — restlessness, bedmaking, panting and sometimes shivering. In some Chows, this can start as much as a week beforehand. A more reliable sign of imminent labour is the temperature. During the last week a bitch's temperature is below normal but in the 24 hours before parturition it shows a sharp drop to about 97 or 98°F (36.1-36.6°C). If you take the temperature twice daily at 12 hour intervals for the week before the expected date, you will easily notice this sudden drop. From then on the average duration of first stage labour, during which the neck of the uterus relaxes ready for the birth, is from six to 24 hours. If it lasts a little longer than this, do not get alarmed as long as the signs are getting progressively more intense. If, however, she quietens down instead it would be wise to contact your vet for advice. By the end of this first stage the cervix is fully dilated.

Now begins the second stage of labour and it is time for you to start monitoring the timing of events. Reflex action of straining will occur with the rhythmic contractions of the uterus. There is no definite answer as to how long she should strain. Chows have rather large puppies compared with other breeds of similar size and so the effort needed to expel them is somewhat greater. It may take an hour or two before the first puppy appears, but certainly never leave her for more than six hours without summoning help. Try to remain calm and supportive of her. Do not fuss her — birth is a natural, normal event with which she is likely to cope well. Let her take up her own position for whelping. Some prefer to lie down, some to sit and some to stand. She knows best what is right for her.

Some strong pushes from the bitch, probably accompanied by a yelp or a grunt, should be followed by either the foetal membrane or by the puppy itself. Most births are in anterior presentation (head first) but quite a number are posterior (hind feet first). Both are normal presentations. A breech birth is one where the back end presents first with the hind legs not extended. A breech can cause problems and requires prompt professional help. With a posterior presentation, birth can be slower and you may have to assist by gripping the hind legs with a towel and exerting a gentle pull downwards and backwards with the strains of the bitch. The puppy may be still inside its membrane sac. If so, a speedy release of the head is needed or it will suffocate. Some Chows will attend to the puppy themselves but many require your help. Since speed is so important at this stage, I usually release the puppy from the membrane myself. Hopefully the puppy will come still attached to the afterbirth by the umbilical cord. Never pull the cord away from the puppy or you could cause an umbilical hernia. I prefer to sever the cord myself, since some bitches get carried away and sever it too close to the puppy. Before I sever the cord, I thoroughly dry the puppy with rough towelling and get it breathing. Do not be afraid to rub strongly. The puppy is not as delicate as you may think and strong rubbing encourages the breathing and stimulates the circulation. Make sure the nose and mouth are clear of mucous. If there is a fear that fluid has been ingested, hold the puppy firmly upside down and shake or swing it. Once the puppy is breathing normally, attend to the cord. Tie it very tightly about 2in (5cm) from the tummy with the button thread, then sever it between the tie and the afterbirth with sterile scissors. Briefly examine it for its sex. Now you can replace it with the bitch near her teats if she so wishes. This will encourage a normal hormonal release within the dam which assists the birth of the next whelp. Some bitches either do not want to know at this time, are clumsy or have a difficult one coming along. If so, then place the puppy in the box you have ready with the covered hot water bottle and loosely cover it with a light blanket until a suitable time comes to give it to its mother. Do not worry because your puppy has a pink tongue. This is perfectly

normal. The characteristic blueness will come, spreading gradually over the tongue in the next few weeks.

The time between births is very variable. The important thing to watch is that straining does not last for too long. Consistent straining for over an hour without producing can mean problems. It is quite common for the last puppy to be born after several hours rest. If the whelping seems to go on for some time, then offer the bitch a drink of warm milk and glucose. Keep a count of the afterbirths. This information will be useful to your veterinarian if there is any thought that she has retained any. Retained afterbirths will make her very ill. The bitch may well wish to devour the afterbirths. This is a natural occurence. It is good for her to eat one or two since they are very high in protein, but too many will give her diarrhoea.

Try to encourage the bitch to leave her litter and go outside to relieve herself when the litter is complete. If she goes outside before you are sure the litter is complete, do watch her in case she strains again outdoors and drops a puppy. Whilst she is outdoors after the completion of her litter, do a very speedy tidy and clean up of her whelping box, for whelping is a messy business, so that she can return to it clean and tidy. Upon her return it may be necessary to persuade her to lie down comfortably to feed her puppies and also to put the puppies to the teats yourself. Very soon instinct takes over and she becomes the proud and capable mother of the best puppies that have ever been born (in her opinion at least!).

The puppies may be noisy for the first few hours but they will soon quieten when their little tummies are satisfied. Happy, healthy puppies are quiet and contented, only crying strongly when they cannot find their mum. This healthy cry is quite different from the weak, grizzly mewing like a seagull which means a sickly

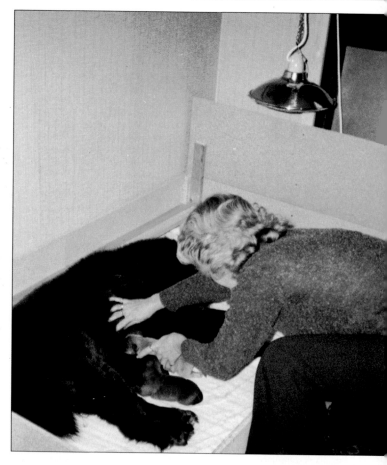

puppy.

Give the new canine family peace, quietness and privacy. Keep a quiet but constant check yourself but firmly discourage all other visitors, including family, for at least 48 hours. Do not, yourself, leave them unattended for long periods — keep a constant check including the night-time period. You will soon learn how confident and capable your bitch is and when to leave her to cope for longer periods of time.

THE NURSING BITCH

After whelping it is quite normal for the bitch to have diarrhoea for the first few days. It is also normal for her to have a discharge from the vulva for two to three weeks. At first this is dark but it gradually fades before ceasing. Keep her as clean as possible with a dilute disinfectant and a sponge, drying her on a towel before she returns to her litter. If the discharge becomes offensive and greenish in colour combined with a rise in her temperature, then something is wrong and you need to call your veterinarian.

Eclampsia

If you find that your bitch is showing signs of panting, shaking or restlessness or she appears to be staggering or have rigid muscles it is possible she has eclampsia. This is a very serious and dangerous condition caused by

Left: A new-born puppy is encouraged to feed by being placed at the teat. The first born is already suckling.

a lack of calcium. It can be cured by an intravenous injection of calcium given by your veterinarian but the condition requires urgent immediate treatment since otherwise it is fatal.

Feeding

A lactating bitch is producing an enormous amount of new body weight and tissue. Each puppy is gaining rapidly. From about two to four weeks old each Chow puppy is gaining nearly 2lb (907g) a week. It therefore follows that it is difficult to overfeed the nursing bitch. She needs plenty of good, nutritious food and regular drinks of milk and glucose. Plenty of water is essential. Keep up the extra vitamin, calcium and mineral supplements.

THE FIRST WEEKS

During the first weeks healthy puppies need little attention beyond a check to make sure that they do not get lost behind mum and making certain that all are getting their fair shares at the 'milk bar'. Their toiletting will be attended to by their mother.

The well fed puppy will double its weight in the first eight to ten days. A normal, healthy puppy has a twitching action when asleep. This seems to disappear after about four weeks. Their eyes will open at around 10-16 days. From the start they should be beady-black since any lightness at this stage will, in all likelihood, be the precursor of a light eye in the adult. They can hear at about 14 days and they get up on rather wobbly legs at about three weeks. By four weeks they are running everywhere! When they can see and hear it is important to start their socialization by getting them used to the sound of your voice and to being handled.

WEANING

It is time to start weaning around the third or fourth week, depending on the number of puppies in the litter and the general health and condition of the dam. I have found that the easiest way is to introduce them to a little scraped raw beef on my fingers. This encourages them to realize that there is another way of feeding as well as the one they have been used to. They quickly catch on and can soon be introduced to the delights of a meal of warm milk and baby cereal. At first more will go over the puppy and everywhere else than down its throat. But fear not, their mother will delightedly clean up the puppies and also finish up any remaining food. Every couple of days another meal can be introduced, the puppies progressing quickly on to four milky meals a day. By five weeks they should be able to eat gravy-soaked puppy meal of best quality with best quality minced meat for two of their meals, the other two meals being of baby cereal, puppy milk or goat's milk (do not use cow milk replacer) and glucose. To one of these meals a day add a complete vitamin, calcium and mineral supplement. Clean drinking water must also be available. Vary the diet by gradually introducing other foods — scrambled egg, chicken, rice pudding, pilchards, white fish, etc. Increase the quantity as the puppies grow and as they depend more and more on the food you give them rather than on their mother's milk. Try to feed them in separate dishes since it is easier to keep an eye on what each puppy devours.

During this weaning period the dam should be separated from her puppies for longer and longer periods of time. At this time some bitches follow their natural instincts of regurgitating food for their puppies. As long as there are no large lumps of food in this, there is no harm done. It is merely nature's way of weaning the litter.

Left: *A very maternal Cedar with her puppies. The puppy bitch's ears are already on the way up in advance of her brother's.*

ROUTINE CARE

Keep a weekly check on the puppies' nails. They can grow very long at this time and cause pain to the bitch. They are soft enough to cut with a pair of nail scissors or clippers. Just tip them a little only and you will cause no pain or bleeding.

Puppies carry roundworms and should be wormed with a safe puppy-strength liquid vermifuge at six weeks according to the directions on the bottle.

Toilet training is usually no problem with Chows since they like to be clean. They will be using their newspaper as a toilet. You will find that you can never have too many newspapers!

Daily grooming can be started from three weeks and must continue until they are ready to leave you at eight weeks. It is only a very few minutes each but the training involved (including mouth and ear inspection) will hold them in good stead all their lives.

Introduction to life outdoors is very dependent upon the weather and the time of year. Never allow young puppies to get wet and cold.

READY TO LEAVE

At eight weeks old, your puppies are ready to leave home and start life with their new family. Check out your prospective buyers carefully. Are their premises suitable? Are they temperamentally the right people to own a Chow? Do they want the puppy for the right reasons? If so, make sure you give them all the help they require: a diet sheet, a pedigree, the Kennel Club registration (if it is back) and a promise to give ongoing help.

If you have bred a sound, happy, healthy puppy which will add to people's pleasure in living, you have done a good job.

Chapter Seven

HEALTH CARE

Basically the Chow is a naturally strong, healthy dog. Apart from routine veterinary visits for inoculation boosters, most Chows pay only rare visits to the surgery. Much health care is a matter of home routine checks which take only a few minutes to do, plus your careful observation of anything which appears to be abnormal for your own dog. Caring owners know their own dogs best and it is upon their careful observation that the veterinarian relies for background information to any symptoms.

ROUTINE CARE

Inoculations It is most important that you take your puppy to have a full course of inoculations to protect him against Distemper (Hardpad), Infectious Canine Hepatitis, Leptospirosis and Parvovirus. For the first few weeks

Below: *Always make sure that your dog's course of protective inoculations is up to date. He really didn't feel the prick.*

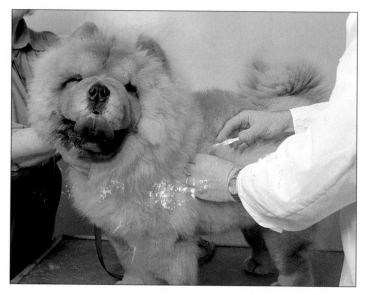

of life the puppy is protected by antibodies gained from his mother. Take your veterinarian's advice as to the age of first inoculation, since some prefer to start the course earlier than others. Certainly the commencement of the course should not be delayed beyond the age of 12 weeks. Until the course is completed the puppy must not be taken outside for walks or be in contact with other dogs, even from the same household, which could have been in contact with an infection. Never forget that the inoculation will require a booster once a year for continual effectiveness.

Nails Some Chows do not wear their nails down naturally. These will need attention by clipping back with canine nail clippers. Take great care not to take off too much. Inside the nail is the quick, a living section which will bleed if cut and will be very painful too. Light coloured nails are easy since you can see the darker quick inside the

nail and can avoid it. Black nails are much more difficult. You have to guess and it is better to err on the side of taking off too little than to cut into the quick. Do watch the front dew claws since, having nothing to wear them down, they can tend to grow too long and can even become so long and curved that they enter the leg itself, causing much pain.

Ears A routine inspection of ears will soon show whether or not they are clean. A small amount of light brown, waxy secretion is normal but any unpleasant smell or a dark reddish brown colour or any sign of discomfort with the ear (scratching or shaking the head) means ear problems and you should see your vet. You can float out any surplus wax with warm olive oil but do not poke around inside ears for you can easily do damage.

Worming Dogs can get roundworm, tapeworm, hookworm, lungworm or whipworm. The first two are the most common. If you suspect that your dog has worms, dose him with either a proprietary brand or with tablets from your veterinarian. It is important that your dog is worm-free, not only for his own health but also because some of these worms can produce problems with children. It is extremely easy and very cheap to keep your animals worm-free.

Diarrhoea This is usually caused by digestive problems. Withhold food for 12 hours but make sure that water is still available. Dose with a little light kaolin (or tablets containing this) and put back on to a bland diet for a while. If diarrhoea persists after 48 hours, take professional advice.

Temperature If you suspect your dog is running a temperature, seek advice immediately. A dog's temperature is normally taken in the rectum but it is not advisable for a novice to try to do this. Take

Below: *The veterinarian is giving this puppy a complete health check before the puppy goes to his new home.*

the dog upon your suspicion and leave the expert to take the temperature.

Giving tablets The easiest way to give your dog tablets is to take about three or four small chunks of cheese and, with your fingers, mould them into little cheese balls. Give at least the first one without it containing any tablet. Insert a tablet into each remaining cheese ball and, hey presto, down they go!

Grass seeds During the summer a Chow can get grass seeds in his coat and between his toes when he is exercising in grass. These need careful removal or they can dig their way into the flesh.

SPECIFIC PROBLEMS

Entropion Unfortunately this is probably one of the most common problems in Chows. It is a hereditary malformation of the eyelids causing the eyelashes to rub on the cornea of the eye. This condition causes much pain to the Chow as is evidenced by eye-blinking, runny eyes (though running eyes may have other causes too) and/or scratching and rubbing the eye. It is surgically correctable, preferably when the dog is fully grown. If, however, a puppy is obviously having problems then your vet will probably prefer not to wait. Some veterinarians have become highly skilled at this operation. Seek the advice of the breeder, who should be told of the problem for their own breeding programme knowledge. It is not the fault of the breeder for, however hard one tries to eradicate it by breeding from clear parents, the problem has come so ingrained that it still can arise. Hopefully, with careful breeding programmes, the situation may get better in future years.

Stifle problems Due to the very straight hind leg and short hock joint, a Chow can damage the cruciate ligament in the hind leg.

The Chow becomes extremely lame. Expert attention is immediately necessary. Here I cannot stress too much that rest and time will be the important factors. Too many people try to hurry the process. Patience is the watchword and care will be needed for many months, not just a few weeks. It is important that during all this long time for healing that the dog is only let out to do the 'necessary' on a controlling collar and lead. I am sure the people passing on the commuter trains at the bottom of my garden must have wondered why I had my Chow on a lead in its own garden being exercised every morning with me in my dressing-gown!

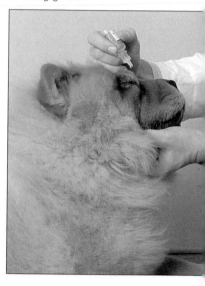

Above: *Prompt veterinary treatment is needed for any eye problem. This Chow had bumped his eye whilst playing.*

Hip Dysplasia The larger breeds of dog, including the Chow, sometimes suffer from an abnormality of the ball and socket joint at the hip. This is not usually seen in young puppies but becomes more evident as they approach maturity. In bad cases it

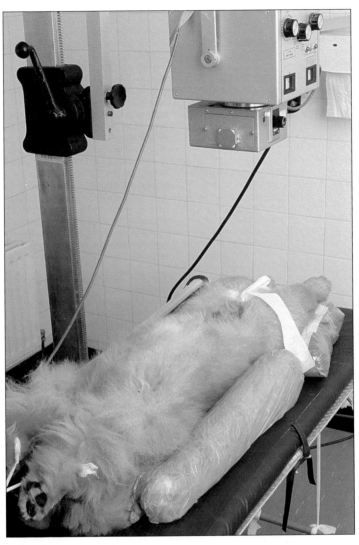

Above: *An anaesthetized Chow in position for a BVA/KC screening hip X-ray. The dog recovered consciousness shortly after.*

can cause pain and lameness. This condition is partly hereditary but it is also exacerbated by overfeeding of supplements (hence my warnings on these earlier) and by getting too much weight on a dog. In Britain there is a British Veterinary Association/Kennel Club scheme for screening this malformation. Once your Chow is over 12 months old you can have him X-rayed to find out the state of his hips if you wish. As long as a breeder has done their best to breed clear of this fault, that is all you can expect.

The precise manner of inheritance of this condition is still under investigation and, like entropion, the mating of two clear specimens does not guarantee a clear puppy.

Anaesthetics The Chow used to be a very difficult subject for anaesthesia. Fortunately, science has advanced and this is now a much safer procedure.

Heat Stroke If your Chow becomes overheated, it is essential to cool his body temperature by the quickest means available. Dunking in cold water, ice cubes, or even surrounding him with frozen food — anything to cool him quickly. Ten minutes of application should be sufficient or you may lower his temperature too far. Even if he recovers quickly, he requires a veterinary check-up. The moral here is DO NOT LEAVE YOUR DOG IN A CAR ON A HOT DAY!

Eczema There are several causes of skin problems. The first one to investigate with a Chow is that you may be giving too much meat protein. This is the most common cause of eczema problems in the breed. If this proves not to be the cause, then there is probably an allergy of some kind. It takes quite a time to investigate the cause, which can be anything from carpets to grass. Proprietary creams and powders can be tried, also there are special shampoos which may help. Try to keep your Chow from tearing the irritating place to pieces and making it worse. I have one bitch who has a problem like this and I have to resort to putting her into an old blouse of mine which, being stripey, I call her 'pyjamas'! But it works and the places heal. Eczema is a question of trial and error but, whilst trying to find the cure, it is possible to calm down the irritation and pain when it occurs. Your veterinarian can give you some tablets to help to stop the irritation.

Bloat Overfeeding, particularly with dry foods, can cause the stomach to blow up, twist and kill. It can also occur if you feed soaked meal which has not been soaked properly. The dog's stomach is blown up and is as tight as a drum skin. It is essential to get expert help immediately. Even a delay of seconds can make all the difference between life and death.

Pyometra This is due to an accumulation of fluid in the uterus and usually occurs about one or two months after the bitch has been in season. Signs are that she is drinking excessively and has abdominal tension. An open pyometra will also show a thick, reddish-brown discharge coming from the vulva. The discharge has a specific and offensive smell.

Below: *With a little ingenuity it is possible to help eczema to heal — even when it means putting on her 'pyjamas'!*

Once smelt you will never forget what that smell means. An emergency operation is usually necessary.

Cystitis Frequent urination which often includes blood needs investigation by the veterinarian. There are several causes of this which can only be expertly diagnosed. Take a urine sample with you. Sometimes this problem can be quickly cured; occasionally it is very persistent.

Wounds Try to deal with any bleeding wound. Use a pad of cotton wool soaked in cold water and apply it with pressure by means of a towel or bandage to the point of bleeding. If the wound appears to be deep, it may need stitching by your vet.

Poisoning If you suspect your dog has been poisoned, the first thing to do is to try to make him sick. A drink of salt and water will act as a speedy emetic. If, however, he has swallowed a corrosive substance do not give an emetic but give a drink of milk to coat the stomach. Get to the veterinarian as soon as possible. If there is anything around which you suspect may have caused the problem, take it with the dog immediately to the vet. The most common causes are slug bait and rat poison. Be careful — if you must use these, keep them well away from any possible contact with animals.

Stings Wasps, bees and mosquitoes can and do sting dogs. If your dog tries to snap at them he may get stung in the mouth. If the sting is visible, remove it with tweezers. Apply a saline solution. If the inside of the mouth or the eyelid begins to swell badly, take your dog to the veterinarian, since he may well require an anti-histamine injection. Speed is essential since a severe swelling in the mouth could lead to respiratory problems.

Fleas This is one problem which does not occur with most Chows. Fortunately, fleas seem to be

Above: Two happy, healthy Chows, imitating the lions in Trafalgar Square, saying, "How much longer do we have to baby-sit?"

unable to get through a Chow's dense undercoat and so a Chow with fleas is a rarity. If, however, your Chow does get fleas they can be difficult to eradicate due to the dense coat they have penetrated. There is an excellent flea spray on the market which you can obtain from your veterinarian and it has an accompanying spray for all bedding, carpets and furniture. Remember, for every flea on the

A schedule of regular health checks	
Daily	Eyes — for excessive discharge and for clarity of sight Faeces — for consistency, colour and frequency
Weekly	Ears — for discharge or smell, also the ear flap for wounds Paws — for wounds, cracks, cysts or nail infections
Monthly	Skin/Coat for abrasions, eczema, lumps, etc. Nails — for length, splitting, inflammation
Six-monthly	Mammary glands — for tumours Dogs: penis — for discharge or wounds; testicles — for any abnormality Bitches: vulva — for abnormal discharge.
Annually	Booster vaccinations

A canine first aid kit

Disinfectant
Nail clippers
Scissors
Tweezers
Old tights (for use as emergency muzzle)
Cotton wool
Children's paracetamol (analgesic) or give a small dose of aspirin
Antiseptic cream
Antiseptic powder
Roll of wide plaster
Roll of bandage of the type that sticks to itself
Roll of crepe bandage
Antihistamine spray (for stings not near mouth or eyes)
Glucose powder
Light Kaolin powder
Gripe mixture
Travel sickness tablets
Eye cream (from vet)
Clinical thermometer (digital read-out)
Worm tablets or liquid
5ml plastic syringe without a needle (from vet)
Miniature of brandy (for the dog!)

---

dog there are another three somewhere around off the dog! Luckily with Chows, fleas are a rare problem.

Kennel Cough This is a virus usually picked up at shows or at boarding kennels. The symptoms are rather like a mild influenza with a persistent cough. It can be treated with antibiotics and usually takes about three or four weeks to subside. During this time, exercise must be kept to being very gentle. It is a highly infectious virus. It is not usually a serious ailment, except in young puppies and elderly dogs. There is a vaccine against Kennel Cough and many boarding kennels insist that you must have your dog vaccinated before they will accept him.

Rabies Due to the quarantine regulations, rabies is not a problem in Britain. In the USA and on the Continent, rabies inoculations are required. Puppies can be given their first rabies inoculation at three months and a second one a year later. This then lasts for three years. If you are exporting from Britain you must get information from the Ministry of Agriculture, Fisheries and Food on the current requirements for inoculations according to the country to which you are exporting.

GENERAL

Do not be afraid of the list of ailments you have just read. Remember that the Chow is basically a very healthy dog, paying only rare visits to the veterinarian. Prevention is better than cure, so a constant watchfulness for the unusual in your dog pays dividends. Do not get your Chow too fat and lazy. A Chow should be an active animal. If he is fed on the best but not overfed, given exercise but not over-exercised, and kept warm and comfortable without being pampered, he is well on the way to being a happy dog. Your Chow is an important member of your family and your loyal and unwavering friend. Treat him well and he will always greet you with joy. As the American Capt Will Judy once said, 'A dog is the only true love that money can buy.'

Appendix

Glossary of Canine Terminology

Affix: A word registered with the Kennel Club which is written before the puppy's name to denote the breeder. May only be used by the owner of the affix.

Almond eye: Eye shaped in a narrow triangle with the short side next to the muzzle.

Angulation: Angle formed by two adjoining bones, particularly the shoulder, forearm, hip joint, stifle and hock.

Anus: Anterior opening under the tail.

Bad mouth: Teeth crooked, misaligned, overshot or undershot.

Balance: Correctly proportioned animal with one part in regard to another.

Barrel ribs: Ribs which are so rounded as to interfere with the elbow action.

Benched show: A show at which the dogs are at rest leashed on benches.

Bitch: Female dog.

Bodied up: Well developed.

Brace Class: A class for two matching dogs belonging to the same owner.

Breechings: The hair on the hindquarters.

Brisket: The part of the lower chest which includes the breastbone.

Brood bitch: A bitch kept for breeding.

Canines: The two upper and two lower large pointed teeth next to incisors.

Castrate: Surgical removal of the testicles.

Champion: A dog which has won three Challenge Certificates under different judges in the UK, sufficient points at major shows in the USA or sufficient CACs on the Continent.

Cobby: Short-bodied and compact.

Conformation: The structure and form of the framework in comparison with the requirements of the breed standard.

Couplings: The area between the last rib and the haunch.

Cow hocked: Hocks turned towards each other.

Cryptorchid: A male dog with neither testicle descended.

Culottes: The hair on the hindquarters.

Dam: Mother of the puppies.

Dew claw: Extra claw on the inside lower portion of legs.

Dog show: An exhibition at which dogs are judged in accordance with an established standard of perfection for each breed.

Double coat: Undercoat plus longer outer coat.

Down at pastern: Weak at front wrist.

Down faced: Tip of nose below level of stop.

Dudley nose: Off-colour nose, light brown or pink.

Elbow: The joint at the top of the forelegs.

Entropion: A condition in which the eyelid turns inward and the lashes irritate the eyeball.

Expression: The general appearance of all features of the head as typical of the breed.

Flank: The body area between the last rib and the hip.

Flews: The inside of the lips.

Gait: A style of movement.

Heat: An alternative word for 'season' in bitches.

Height: Vertical measurement from the top of the shoulder to the ground.

Hip dysplasia: Malformation of the hip joint.

Hock: Lower joint of the hind legs.

In-breeding: The mating of very closely related dogs.

Incisors: The upper and lower front teeth between the canines.

In season: On heat; ready for mating.

Layback: The angle of the shoulder blade vertically against the rib-cage, and/or the angle to the horizontal.

Level bite: Incisors meeting edge to edge.

Line breeding: The mating of related dogs with a common ancestor.

Litter: The puppies from one whelping.

Maiden: An unmated bitch, or a dog or bitch which has never won a first prize except in puppy classes.

Molars: Rear teeth behind the canines (pre-molars are immediately behind the canines).

Monorchid: A male dog with only one testicle descended.

Muzzle: The head in front of the eyes, including nose, nostrils and jaws.

Oestrus: Another word for 'season' or 'heat'.

Overshot: The upper incisors overlapping the lower incisors at too great a distance to touch them.

Pastern: Foreleg between the carpus and the digits (wrist).

Patella: Knee cap composed of cartilage at the stifle joint.

Pigmentation: Blue-black colouring of tongue, flews and roof of mouth; black colour of gums, nose leather and nails; darkness of the iris of the eye.

Pinning: The turning in of the front feet when in action.

Puppy: A dog up to 12 months of age.

Quality: Refinement and finesse.

Quarters: The two hind legs.

Register: To record with the Kennel Club the details of a dog's breeding.

Roach back: A convex curvature of the spine towards the loin.

Scissor bite: A close overlap of upper teeth over the lower teeth, the inside of the upper incisors touching the outside of the lower incisors.

Self-colour: A matching colour to the coat colour.

Set on: The angle of attachment of tail or ears.

Set up: Posed so as to make the most of the dog's appearance for the show ring.

Shaded: Lighter colouring on tail and hindquarters.

Silver shaded: White shadings on the tail and hindquarters of a black dog.

Sire: The father of the puppies.

Slab-sided: Rib cage lacking curvature.

Snipy: Muzzle pointed and weak.

Spay: Surgical removal of the ovaries and uterus.

Splay feet: Feet with toes spread wide.

Spring of ribs: Curvature of ribs for heart and lung capacity.

Stance:	Manner of standing.
Standard:	A word picture of perfection for the breed.
Stifle:	The knee joint of the hind leg, particularly relating to the inner side.
Stop:	The depression between and in front of the eyes.
Straight hocks:	Hocks that are in correct vertical line.
Stud:	Male used for breeding.
Stud Book:	A Kennel Club book recording pedigrees of winning dogs.
Topline:	The outline from behind the withers to the tail set.
Trousers:	The hair on the hindquarters.
Undershot:	The lower incisors projecting or overlapping the upper incisors.
Weaving:	The crossing of front or hind legs when in action.
Well let down:	Having short hocks.
Well sprung:	Roundness or curvature of the rib cage.
Whelping:	The act of giving birth.
Withers:	The highest point of the shoulders, well behind the neck.
Wry mouth:	Lower jaw does not line up with upper jaw.

Abbreviations

AI:	Artificial insemination.
AKC:	American Kennel Club.
ANKC:	Australian National Kennel Council.
AOC:	Any other colour (than red in UK).
AVNSC:	Any variety not separately classified.
B:	Bitch.
BIS:	Best in Show.
BOB:	Best of Breed.
BOS:	Best Opposite Sex.
CAC:	Certificat d'aptitude au Championnat de Beauté.
CACIB:	Certificat d'aptitude au Championnat International de Beauté.
CC:	Challenge Certificate.
Ch:	Champion.
CKC:	Canadian Kennel Club.
D:	Dog.
FCI:	Federation Cynologique Internationale.
HD:	Hip Dysplasia.
Int Ch:	International Champion.
JW:	Junior Warrant.
KC:	Kennel CLub (UK).
KUSA:	Kennel Union of South Africa.
LOF:	Livres des Origines Francais (French Stud Book).
LOSH:	Livre Origines St Hubert (Belgian Stud Book).
NAF:	Name applied for.
Nordic Ch:	Nordic Champion.
P:	Puppy.
Res CC:	Reserve Challange Certificate.
TAF:	Transfer applied for.

Breed Clubs in Britain

Chow Chow Club; Chinese Chow Chow Club; Chow Chow Club of Scotland; Chow Chow Club of Wales; Midland Chow Chow Club; National Chow Chow Club; Northern Counties Chow Chow Club; North Eastern Chow Chow Club; West of England Chow Chow Club.

Addresses of secretaries of these clubs can be obtained from the Kennel Club.

Breed Clubs in the Rest of the World

Addresses of secretaries of breed clubs may be obtained from the appropriate country's Kennel Club.

Kennel Clubs

Australia	Australian National Kennel Council, Royal Show Grounds, Ascot Vale, Victoria.
Belgium	Societe Royale Saint-Hubert, Avenue de l'Armee, 25. B-1040. Brussels.
Canada	Canadian Kennel Club, 2150 Bloor Street West, Toronto, M6S 1M8. Ontario.
France	Societe Centrale Canine, 215, Rue St Denis, 75083 Paris. Cedex 02.
Germany	Verband fur das Deutsche Hundewesen (VDH). Postfach 1390, 46 Dortmund.
Holland	Raad van Beheer op Kynologisch Gebied in Nederland. Emmalaan 16, Amsterdam.Z.
Ireland	Irish Kennel Club. 23 Earlsfort Terrace, Dublin 2.
Italy	Ente Nazionale Della Cinofilia Italiana, Viale Premuda. 21 Milan.
New Zealand	New Zealand Kennel Club. Private Bag, Porirua, New Zealand.
South Africa	Kennel Union of South Africa, 6th Floor, Bree Castle, 68 Bree Street, Cape Town 8001.
Spain	Real Sociedad Central de Fomento de las razas en Espana, Los Madrazo 20, Madrid 14.
United Kingdom	The Kennel Club, 1-4 Clarges St, London W1Y 8AB.
USA	American Kennel Club, 51 Madison Avenue, New York 10010.
	The United Kennel Club Inc. 100 East Kilgore Rd, Kalamazoo, M1 49001-5598.